BACKYARD HARVEST

BACKYARD HARVEST

by

Marjorie Blanchard

BOBBS-MERRILL
INDIANAPOLIS / NEW YORK

Copyright © 1978 by Marjorie Page Blanchard

All rights reserved including the right of reproduction
in whole or in part in any form
Published by The Bobbs-Merrill Company, Inc.
Indianapolis   New York

Library of Congress Cataloging in Publication Data
Blanchard, Marjorie P
Backyard harvest.
Includes index.
1. Cookery (Fruit)   2. Fruit-culture.   I.   Title.
TX811.B64   641.6′4   77–15447
ISBN 0–672–52299–3

Designed by Helen Barrow
Drawings by Christine Swirnoff
Manufactured in the United States of America

First printing

ACKNOWLEDGMENTS

I wish to thank the Agricultural Extension Services throughout the United States for all of the invaluable information they so willingly provided, and give special thanks to Ed Rose of Stauffer, Don Ourecky in Geneva, New York, and all of the experts at Parlier, California, who were so generous with their time and advice.

*To my husband and two children,
who have worked as hard as I have on this book*

CONTENTS

INTRODUCTION

Harvesting from one's own backyard can go from dreamy contemplation in mid-winter to reality in the spring and fruitful enjoyment in the bountiful months of bearing. Perhaps the moment has come, in these uneasy times, to have a more basic realization of self-sufficiency. Instead of planting decorative shrubbery for landscaping purposes alone, wouldn't it be more sensible to plant bushes and trees and hedges that contribute to our food production as well as the beautification of our property?

You might start by lining the driveway with fruit trees, picking a variety of fruits and considering their culinary value as you choose different kinds. For instance, don't succumb to Delicious and McIntosh apples just because they are familiar.

Those you can pick up anywhere. Try some of the older and rarer types such as Gravenstein and Spitzenberg and Russet. They are infinitely more interesting and better for muffins, pies and tortes. Plant the white peach for juicy eating out of hand; the golden peaches for puddings and a rum marmalade. Plums are generally ignored by home gardeners and we tend to buy only those we see in the market, which are of limited variety. There are many others, including a golden plum that makes a beautiful *kuchen* or cake.

If your driveway is short, work out a plan for a small orchard to take care of the rest of your fruit trees, including apricot, pear and fig. A sunny wall is the perfect spot for an espaliered pear tree—the nicest thing that could happen to such a perfect flowering tree.

Perhaps the one thing that makes us realize the great size of this country we live in is the wide variety of foods that are grown in its wide-open spaces. Those who live in the North drink orange juice, eat grapefruit and occasionally venture to try the orange-fleshed persimmon or the leathery looking papaya, but it is hard to imagine these fruits gracing anyone's own backyard. And yet, there are quite a few fruits that can be attempted with success in a semitropical climate. The glossy leaves of the citrus tree are a common sight throughout the warmer states and many home orchardists are having fun with the mango, persimmon and papaya as well.

Strawberries grow in a bed and raspberries grow in a patch —both ideally accessible to the kitchen so that no time will be lost between picking and preparing these fruits for eating, either with heavy cream and sugar or piled at the last moment into a snowy meringue shell.

Blackberries belong in a hedgerow. They will keep out all intruders with their spiky thorns, attract bees with their perfect white flowers and please the cook as they meld into a sugary deep-dish pie. The kissin' kin of the blackberry are the dewberry and the boysenberry. Who could resist planting a bush that bears the delightful name of Lucretia Dewberry?

Gooseberries and currants have had to live down a blot upon their good name due to the distressing fact that both of them could be carriers of a disease called white pine blister. This disease does not affect the berry bushes but could decimate a stand of white pine trees. Thanks to modern medicine, this scourge has been controlled and there are now only five states that will not allow the importation of the gooseberry and the currant. So it is time to reevaluate the visual and culinary beauty of these worthwhile fruits.

So many fashions are cyclical and foods are no exception. The mention of elderberries and mulberries could start a flood of reminiscences ranging from "deep mulberry-dyed tea gowns" to the intricate processes of home wine making. They do deserve a place in your planning, for whatever reason.

The highbush blueberry is decorative as well as edible, with shiny green leaves that turn to flame in the fall, and it could well be used as screening for a play yard. Put in enough for the children, the birds and lots of pies and pancakes.

An old-fashioned grape arbor, or just a trellis, lends a romantic note to anyone's backyard and, before the grapes are ready for jelly, juice or wine, the large-veined leaves make pretty liners for picnic baskets and fruit platters. You might also try brining your own grape leaves when they are young and tender for use in Dolmas, those fascinating Greek-inspired packages of lamb, rice and pine nuts.

These are just a few of the ways in which you can make your own backyard into a self-indulgent greengrocer's. The possibilities are endless and I shall explore them individually in the following chapters. To start thinking along the right lines, concentrate on the apple section in Chapter 1. It will describe the basic procedures involved in all orchard planting.

PART ONE

The Orchard

*"From whence sprang this perfect fruit,
This peach so fair of rosy blush?"*

Poets, lyricists and artists have all used the fruits of the orchard to symbolize beauty, love and perfection. Their claims may be exaggerated in romantic fashion, but it is certainly true that an orchard in the spring is a beautiful sight and the perfect setting for a lover's tryst or even a wedding. I remember a gazebo fashioned from espaliered pear trees that was used for a late spring wedding. The trees had been planted when the bride was an infant and, luckily for the orchardist, the story ended happily.

There we have one good reason for planting an orchard: sheer beauty. However, as this same scene could be set with nonfruiting trees as well, the main reason for cultivating your orchard has to be a practical one: you like the availability of

17

fresh fruit, when you want it and where you want it. We planted our first orchard for just one fruit—the Georgia Belle peach. It is white-fleshed, sweet, and perfect for eating out of hand, but because they do not ship well, these delicate peaches are not readily available in the North. The answer seemed to be to grow our own. One tree does not make an orchard and, considering nature's basic requirements, it doesn't even make half an orchard so, as one tree led to another, a small but fairly well-rounded orchard was the result. Then came the year we had a bumper crop of cherries. The orchard was suddenly the perfect place for a party with wine and cheese and cherries; "pick your own" was our slogan.

If you need more convincing reasons for establishing an orchard, consider your own contribution to reforestation. Drive around the countryside and look at the neglected orchards; be reminded of the thousands of apple trees that were cut down by the fiery axe of Prohibition. Or simply follow the example of a seventy-two-year-old man who is replanting his fruit trees for the enjoyment of those who will follow, and who sincerely believes that those who are close to nature live longer and more fruitful lives.

As with any project you initiate yourself, you can have exactly what you want. Fruits of all kinds can be yours, including those that are hard to find in the markets—some of the older and rarer apples, the more unusual varieties of peaches and pears, plums in all colors (not just purple), golden apricots, perhaps an old-fashioned quince (whose branches can be cut and forced to bloom inside while the snow is still on the ground), a fig grown in a tub. Catalogs glow with praise and pictures, but find out from a professional grower or your local extension service which fruits do well in your own geographical area. Some are labeled hardy and indeed they are, but they still won't produce as well as you might like.

Pick your location, then draw a plan. This does not require any great artistic talent; just some graph paper, a ruler and

PLAN FOR A SMALL BACKYARD

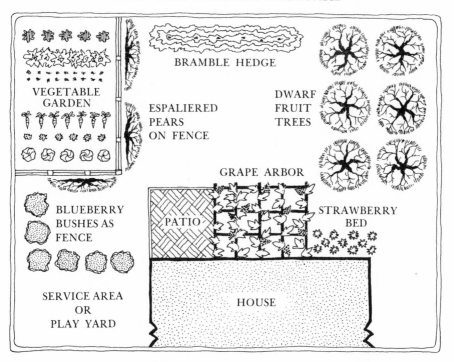

BRAMBLE HEDGE

VEGETABLE
GARDEN

ESPALIERED
PEARS
ON FENCE

DWARF
FRUIT
TREES

GRAPE ARBOR

BLUEBERRY
BUSHES AS
FENCE

PATIO

STRAWBERRY
BED

SERVICE AREA
OR
PLAY YARD

HOUSE

a sharp pencil. When planning your planting, location is all important. In your drive around the countryside, notice that many orchards are placed high on a windy hill. There are good reasons for this. Frost settles in low pockets and fruit trees should be up and away from an unexpected nip from nature at the wrong time of year. Hills also mean good drainage and lots of sun. These are essential qualifications for any edible planting area, high or low.

The size trees you plant depends largely on the amount of space you have. Thanks to research done by professional orchardists, we amateurs can go into the fruit-growing business in a small and personal way, using dwarf and semidwarf trees. They are much easier to cope with than the full-sized fruit trees and they bear prolifically. The necessary tasks of spraying, pruning and so on (and these *are* necessary) are not such an awesome chore when done on a small scale.

It is helpful to visit a nursery and see the trees at their various stages of growth because one of the most important things to remember when planning is to allow enough space between trees. To produce well, a fruit tree needs air and sunlight and room to expand. On your paper plan, you should allow about 10 to 12 feet between each dwarf tree, and 15 to 18 feet between each semidwarf. Count on two or more trees per type of fruit and try to achieve an interesting variety, with some early, some mid-season and some late-ripening fruits. If you do everything right and you're born lucky, you'll be eating fruit off your own bushes and trees from early spring through late fall.

Going back to our own first orchard, we put in eighteen trees and did not lose one. The only serious mistake we made has turned out to be an interesting botanical error. We planted a pear tree, and every spring it was the loveliest tree in the orchard, its bloom outdoing all the others. Each fall we looked in vain for pears. None. Then one autumn day my husband came into the house with a basketful of crabapples. Neither of us remembered ordering a crabapple tree. We hadn't. The spring pear produces crabapples in the fall. We had made the mistake of planting too deep, covering the graft so the tree reverted to its original rootstock, which was crabapple. It makes for good conversation as well as good crabapple jelly, although we do miss the pears.

CHAPTER 1

HARDY FRUIT TREES

APPLES

Whether or not Eve gave an apple to Adam, this well-rounded fruit has graced mankind's table for a long, long time. It seems to symbolize health, prosperity and good living in general. From the golden apples of the Greeks to the reddening orchards of Johnny Appleseed, apples have played their part in history, culinary and otherwise. Apples even have their medicinal uses. We have all been brought up on the adage, "An apple a day keeps the doctor away." Now it seems that apples are good tranquilizers as well. A recent study shows that the apple a day also calms the nerves and lessens the frequency of headaches—another good reason for putting in at least a couple of apple trees.

When we realize the tremendous variety of apples available to us today—over a thousand kinds—it is hard to believe that at one time on this continent there were only crabapples. This is why the early colonists called all of their cider apples "crabs." But the settlers brought seeds with them and it wasn't long before they had many to choose from, including some that we no longer see today. Think about this when you buy your apple trees. There are so many kinds other than McIntosh and Delicious; apples that are crisper, harder, winier, or more suited to your cooking purposes. Think about what you like to do with apples—which are best for sauce? Which hold up in tarts and pies? Which bake best, either encased in pastry or poached in maple syrup? Which fry into crisp, rosy rings to be served with a glazed pork roast?

To the concerned cook, there is no such thing as the perfect all-around apple. The McIntosh, with its pinkish color, makes good sauce, but it needs the addition of Cortland and Northern Spy for flavor. Rhode Island Greening, a very old apple, makes superb pie, with the addition of lots of sugar and spices. The Cortland does not turn brown after slicing, so it is the obvious choice for a salad or to serve with Stilton cheese and roasted walnuts. Rome apples are known to be the best bakers and, when ripe, resemble every pictorial replica of an apple you've ever seen. There are summer apples, early fall apples, mid-season and late-season apples. There are apples with romantic names such as Honeygold, Holly, Chenango Strawberry and Poundsweet. Spitzenberg was reputedly Thomas Jefferson's favorite. Winter Banana has a distinctly banana aroma and the Golden Russet is an old variety that is no longer grown commercially at all.

Pomology—the science and practice of growing fruit—is a fascinating subject and there is research being done the year 'round on developing new strains of apples through cross-breeding. Send for a lot of catalogs and then, if possible, take a trip to your state agricultural experiment station. They will advise you on what apple trees will do best in your area. I was all set to put in a Cox's Orange Pippin because I had eaten one in England and been told that it was one of the finest dessert apples grown. Luckily, I consulted one of Connecticut's leading pomologists and was told that it was a very poor grower here and it would probably be a great disappointment. He then advised me to grow another type that would do better. Take the expert's advice whenever you can.

We are all impatient, but remember that the youngest trees transplant best and they do grow fast. In no time you will be doing a bit of pruning, but don't count on eating for four or five years.

SOIL

There is always an ideal way to do a job and it never hurts to know about it. Sometimes we can take advantage of this particular knowledge and sometimes not. The best way to prepare the ground for any planting is to cover it with hay and let the earth lie fallow for a year. This process kills the weeds and enriches the soil at the same time.

However, most of us are in too much of a hurry to go through this procedure; we want to begin *now*. We have picked out the apple trees we wish to plant; we have walked around our property and decided where the trees will go; we have made a plan on paper and then followed it up by putting sticks in the ground as markers to get an idea of how it will look. We have even thought of having the soil tested. No, this doesn't require a degree in chemistry. It is a very simple procedure that pays off later because you will find out exactly what to feed your land to make it produce with maximum efficiency. Just take six or eight random samples of earth from the area in which you wish to plant and mix them up in one container. Send the container off to your state agriculture experiment station. They will send you back a complete analysis of your soil and advice on what to feed it. Soil analysis is based on its pH factor (acid content). This should be between 6.0 and 6.5 for most fruit trees.

Like everything else that is alive and breathing and wants to grow, fruit trees respond best to ideal conditions. Don't we all? As far as soil goes, these trees prefer an easily worked, deep and well-drained soil with a subsoil that permits the roots to go down—way down. They do not like wet feet, however—a condition caused by poor drainage. If you have a hopeless drainage situation, give up the project. But if you are optimistic enough to believe that there is always a remedy for what looks hopeless, consider the possibility of diverting the surface water away from the site or putting in drainage tile.

The other type of soil that is not ideal for fruit trees is soil with a hardpan (packed soil and gravel) layer down deep in the subsoil. However, here again this can be circumvented by planting the trees above the hardpan and giving them extra water during dry spells. Soil conditions are numbered among the basics, and should be dealt with before you get carried away with visions of a beautiful orchard in full bloom. Here is the spot for another old adage, "An ounce of prevention . . ."

If you already know, or have been advised by experts, that you are the proud possessor of ordinary good garden soil (and whoever thought that dirt would make such a difference in your outlook on life?), and your topsoil has not been removed by an acquisitive contractor, you probably do not need to add fertilizer when planting. However, here are some possible alternative conditions and their remedies, in case your soil is not good.

Clay or hardpan subsoil: Make the hole larger and mix well-rotted cow manure or peat moss with the soil that has been dug out.

Acid soil: This is sour soil and it must be sweetened. The antidote is lime, which is not actually a fertilizer, but ground rock. Some people believe in adding it to any type of soil, as it improves the quality of the fruit.

Sweet soil: Conversely, this soil can be made more acid by adding leaf mold, peat or sawdust.

Sandy soil: Add cow manure and peat moss.

You can see how you may become much better acquainted with the local lumberyard, farmer and nurseryman, and how commonplace items such as sawdust and fireplace ashes will gain exaggerated importance in your life. You will find yourself discussing the merits of various fertilizers at cocktail parties and knowledgeably mentioning "pH factor" to anyone who will listen.

PLANTING

One well-known nursery starts its planting instructions with the large-type warning: "95% OF TREES FAIL DUE TO IMPROPER PLANTING." My own interpretation of these dire words is that receiving fruit trees is very much like taking on a new puppy. It has been perfectly cared for up to this point of delivery to its new home; don't botch the job now.

The word "ideal" keeps cropping up, and we probably overuse it, but if you can start off with man-made ideal conditions in your soil quality, planting, timing, pruning and spraying, then you have given nature a big boost, and it might offset some of her whimsical ways—such as raising the temperature to an unseasonal eighty degrees in the middle of March or springing a late frost just when the branches are budding. These are conditions that will make an orchardist weep tears of frustration, but always hope for better times ahead.

The *ideal* time for planting is early spring, just after the ground thaws and before the plant growth starts.

The day the trees arrive seems to be an emotional high point in our lives. Perhaps because it is a true harbinger of spring—the sign that nature hasn't forgotten, and neither has the nursery. If by any chance the trees arrive without instruction and you cannot plant them immediately, here is what you should do:

If the trees are frozen upon arrival, place them, still in their wrappings, in a cool, dark, frost-free area for 36 to 48 hours so they will thaw slowly. As long as they are not shocked by a sudden change in temperature they will be perfectly all right.

If the ground is still too frozen to dig deep and plant properly, the trees should be "heeled in." Dig a trench in a shaded area where the ground is moist and well-drained. Make the trench big enough to take the roots comfortably, with enough room to wiggle their toes, so to speak. Open the bundle and separate the trees, spreading out the roots. Place the trees with the roots in the trench and the trunks making a forty-five-degree angle with the ground, and with the tops pointing toward the southwest. Now shovel in the dirt loosely over and around the roots, covering up a few inches of trunk. Tamp the earth down to get rid of air pockets, and water if dry. Trees will keep for a month under these conditions. However, your timing really should be better than this. After all, you've waited a long time for this moment.

If conditions are favorable and you are able to plant within two days of arrival, unpack trees and immerse the roots in a tub of water.

For the task of digging there are two essentials—a good shovel and a strong back. The hole should be three times the size of the root ball; this is a sizeable hole, but you must not crowd the tree roots. Another adage: "Never put a five-dollar tree in a fifty-cent hole."

Measure the root ball first; don't keep putting the tree in the hole to see if it will fit. I'll warn you: Dig until you think it *must* be big enough and then dig some more, because it isn't. A tree needs the largest possible area to absorb water and nutrients, all to get a good start on life in what will be its permanent location. It has a lot of work to do producing that bountiful supply of apples each fall.

Put the topsoil to one side. If you have decided that the soil needs anything in the way of nourishment, you can add to it now. *Do not* put manure directly into the hole—if it comes in contact with the bare roots it could burn them, causing irreparable damage to the tree.

At this point, check the roots of the young tree. If they are damaged—that is, torn or broken—a bit of surgery is needed, and you are the only surgeon around at the moment. Take a sharp knife and cut the damaged part off, cutting in a slanting direction on the underside of the root. In this way the wound will heal over easily by throwing out fibrous roots at the end. No, it doesn't have to be painted or taped. Nature will take care of the healing.

Now place the tree in the hole, leaning it slightly facing the wind. It will straighten up as it grows. Be sure to place the graft union one inch above the surface. Incidentally, "graft" is a word that pops up quite often when talking about orchards, so it should be defined. It is the joining union between the trunk's base and root system. Grafting is a means of tying together the two parts that make up a fruit tree to make a new

MODIFIED CLEFT GRAFT

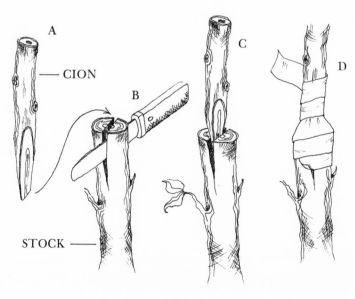

fruit tree, as fruits are not grown from seed in most cases. These two parts are the *stock* and the *cion*. The stock is the plant on which the grafting is done—the paternal forebear, so to speak. The cion is the newcomer who will be brought in as a permanent member of the family. It all might be likened to the old family tree that once had good, strong stock but that now needs a little new blood to keep reproducing strong lines. The easiest, and most interesting, way to become familiar with grafts is to do some grafting yourself.

Back to this first tree that has been waiting patiently to be planted. Spread the roots out gently and, holding the tree with one hand, spread loose soil around the roots with the other. Firm the soil occasionally to prevent air pockets. Then fill the hole to ground level with soil and tamp the earth down firmly. Water the tree well. We leave the hose right on the tree, barely running, while we start on the next planting. Need I mention that we have dug all the holes before unwrapping the trees? (Leave 15 to 20 feet between each hole.) In case you get interrupted in your work or put your back out, at least the holes have been dug and the trees will have a home.

When all the trees are planted and watered, spread any remaining soil loosely around the trunks. Then take a preventive measure that may save you some grief later on. Run a two-foot-high circle of wire mesh around the tree about one foot out from the trunk. This will keep away all those small animals who feast on young bark.

If you have been wondering about fertilizer (some of the garden supply people would have us believe that nothing will grow without it), wait a bit. If your soil is good, or if you have added nutrients to correct a problem, do not fertilize now. Concentrate on mulch and see how the trees do during their first year with you.

MULCHING

For various reasons, trees need mulch. Mulching is the process of covering the area surrounding the tree with protective materials, such as hay, pine needles or pine bark. One reason is to prevent loss of moisture. Another is to give the tree a more constant soil temperature—a bit like an electric blanket. Mulching will not totally stop weeds from growing. What does? But it will keep them down and make them easier to pull out. Mulching also adds necessary nutrition to the soil. Don't forget that weeds must have something to grow on, and that something is the nutrition that rightfully should be going to your trees. In other words, the trees and the weeds are competing for the same food in the soil, and which do you want to win?

Mulch can be peat moss, compost, shredded leaves, straw, chips, chopped corncobs or hay. You might even consider placing hay on the ground between the fruit trees, covering the whole orchard with it. This is not a first-year, or even second-year decision. The decision comes after you realize that there would be a lot less lawn to mow this way and that the tree trunks are being nicked and scraped by the mower blades. A strictly esthetic addition to the area can be made by planting spring bulbs around the base of each tree—a pleasant prelude to the flowering blossoms that will come later.

Whatever you do, be sure to leave a nongrassy area of two to three feet around the base of your trees. The needs of lawns and orchards are not always the same. For example, in the western desert areas a lawn must be watered constantly to keep it going. That would be too much water for most trees, though. In the East, where rainfall is more dependable, we can usually let nature take care of the moisture content of both lawn and orchard. Or perhaps we don't worry as much about the grass as something green seems to come up every year anyhow.

FERTILIZING

This is a subject that can be unbearably technical, and again you might think you need an advanced degree in organic chemistry to handle it. Rest assured. If that were necessary, we would see very few successful home orchards and I would not be encouraging you to attempt it.

Of course, trees that are going to produce fruit for us to eat need the right kind of a diet, and the most important food in that diet is nitrogen. How does the amateur know if his trees need nitrogen? The answer should come easily to those who are parents because it is simply a case of observation. Does the child look pale and listless? Are the leaves a washed-out green and, even more significant, what is the length of the shoot growth of the past season?

Shoot growth (name dropping in the orchard again) can be determined by measuring the area between the scars circling the twigs and the tip of the branch. It signifies how much the tree grew last season, and can average between 10 and 20 inches during the first six years of a tree's life. Then, as is true for children, the growth will taper off and proceed more slowly.

In the early spring—before you think anything could possibly be going on outside, but a little fresh air would be welcome —take a walk in the orchard and look carefully at your trees. Bring along a ruler and measure the shoot-growth length on several trees. Then take an average. This growth is easy to recognize because it is a different color than the older growth —brighter and cleaner looking. If there has not been at least 10 inches of shoot growth, then the aid of nitrogen is in order.

This is probably as good a time as any to recommend a chart for those of you with orderly minds. My husband is a chart maker, thank Heaven, because I am not and yet I appreciate its value. When you come back into the house on that cold Sunday in February or March, feeling optimistic about the

SHOOT GROWTH

SOLID BLACK
INDICATES NEW
GROWTH

chances of spring coming sometime, get out a notebook and start a record of the progress of your first trees. Put down their growth patterns and what you are doing in the way of care and maintenance, including fertilizing, spraying, pruning, etc. You'd be surprised how one forgets from year to year. Try to keep this record for the first few years, at least up to the age of bearing. It will not only help you with any replanting, but it will come in very handy when you are called upon to give advice to the new orchardist in the neighborhood.

Any fertilizing should preferably be done during the dormant season. A lot of growers in colder climates like to spread fertilizer on the snow, the theory being that the melting snow will take the nutrients down into the root system. Certainly you would not wish to fertilize in the fall. The tree would produce a lot of growth that would be nipped by the autumn cold.

I know people who fertilize religiously. I know others who boast that they have never had to fertilize because their "soil is so good." There is a happy medium. My friend with the super soil is concerned now, after six years of relying on that alone, because his fruit production is down. Could it be that the soil is tired? On the other hand, too much of a good thing will cause heavy foliage and poorer quality fruit.

With soil that is good to begin with, an annual application of a mixed fertilizer (such as 10-10-10) or *well-rotted* manure during the dormant season should take care of feeding. We have found that one of the best ways to apply fertilizer is to broadcast it evenly on the ground, starting about halfway between the trunk and the tips of the branches. Extend the spread a bit beyond the tips. If you feel energetic and especially dedicated, you can make small holes 6 inches deep all through this area and place the fertilizer in them. *Do not* use more fertilizer than is recommended. That is, $\frac{1}{4}$ to $\frac{1}{2}$ pound of mixed fertilizer per the tree's year of age. The maximum is 10 pounds per tree. And remember, at this point we are talking about standard apple trees. Other fruits have other requirements.

32

If you still feel in the dark about your soil and its annual needs for food, why not buy a soil-testing kit? They are great fun to use (I managed one successfully with just one year of chemistry behind me), and will keep you in constant touch with what is going on down there. It's a bit like taking your own blood pressure.

PRUNING

Give the average man a pair of pruning shears and he'll give everything in sight a haircut whether it needs it or not. For the first few years, be gentle with your orchard. Following the advice of an old-time orchardist, we didn't prune ours at all for three years in order to let the tree get a good, firm grip on life before we started trimming. However, we live in southern Connecticut where growth is much more limited than in southern California or those states with perfect climates and long growing seasons. This system would not work there.

Why do we prune? The first reason is to produce good fruit and to increase the size of the fruit. Pruning invigorates the tree by getting rid of the dead wood and forcing growth into the younger branches. This is especially true for older trees. Another reason is to expose maximum leaf area to the sunlight; no sun, no fruit. But perhaps the obvious reason for careful, thoughtful pruning and the one easiest to realize is esthetics. The trees take on desirable shape and form when we prune, and are totally under control. Again, as with bringing up children, it pays to establish good habits early in the game. So we'll start with the first pruning—the one you do when you plant the tree.

You are already observing the first rule, which is: Always prune during the dormant season. You have planted the trees during the dormant season; now prune them. If you have bought what are called one-year "whips" (and that's what they resemble) there will not be any side branches. Just prune the tree to a height of 3 feet. Two-year nursery trees may have quite a few side branches. Here is the way to handle this at first con-

33

fusing situation: Prune the trees to a central leader (main trunk). Cut back the side branches to half their original length and remove all broken branches. Remove any branches that form less than a forty-five-degree angle with the main trunk and any branches that are less than 24 inches up from the ground if they are thin and spindly. Leave the larger branches that are lower than 24 inches, but prune them back to 6 inches. The following year remove those stubs. That is enough for now. Put the pruning shears away!

Don't make the mistake common to most amateur orchardists —pruning too heavily. This tends to set back the development of the trees and you will have to wait longer for the fruit. Believe me, the wait before you can pick that first apple is long enough without adding to it.

If the central leader has forked, forming a definite "V" at the top of your tree after the second or third season, retain the side of the V that is growing into the prevailing winds, unless it is definitely the weaker of the two.

When pruning, think about air circulation. The ideal is to have branches going out from the central leader, leaving the center of the tree open to the sun and sky. Cut off all branches that cross each other and all ground suckers (shoots that come up from the roots around the base of the tree). Always cut just above a bud. Look at your tree. It should be pyramid-shaped, not umbrella-shaped. The wood should grow in a horizontal or upright position; fruit-bearing trees should never grow down. Therefore, you should remove a branch at the point where it starts to turn downward.

Once again, you should prune to achieve nearly horizontal branches in a balanced arrangement around the tree. However, you are not painting a picture of a tree on a canvas; you are working with a living entity, and sometimes you must let the tree decide. Think of standing on a hillside and letting the summer breezes blow through your hair and the summer sun warm you all over. The trees are responsive to these same elements of nature.

One final note on the subject. If you insist upon having top-quality, sharp knives in your kitchen, then apply the same standards to the tools you use in the orchard. If not, now's the time to change your ways, in both places. The sharper the knife, the cleaner and smoother the cut. As the trees get older and the branches are larger, these cuts will leave quite sizeable scars. These scars should be painted with orange shellac, grafting wax or special tree paints.

POLLINATION

To get normal fruit crops, you must consider pollination. It is a birds and bees situation with the bees being the most important factor. Honeybees do the work of transferring pollen from one tree to another. However, you have to give them something to work with so be sure you plant more than one variety of apple tree.

There are some trees that are "self-fruitful." These trees will set fruits when pollinated by pollen from their own flowers or another tree of the same variety. Other fruit trees are "self-sterile," either partially or completely. These trees must be pollinated by pollen from a tree of a different variety. When you embarked upon this project, however, it was obviously not in your mind to study and memorize the sex life of the apple tree. The best way to handle the problem is to plant a variety of trees. Then you can be sure that the bees will have something worthwhile to work with. In an average spring nature does take care of all of this, although beekeeping is on the rise with many orchardists. Large commercial orchards often rent out their hives. They are kept for as long as it takes to pollinate the trees and then sent on farther north to be used again. The bees will carry out their assignment as long as you don't get careless with the insecticides. Never spray during bloom. Yes, there are certain fungicides that can be applied, but it is safer to do nothing. Leave nature alone for a while.

INSECTS AND DISEASES

We have naturally wandered into that controversial question—to spray or not to spray. Actually the professionals will tell you that spraying is essential, and they're right. If you want to have fruit production, then you must spray. As a friend said recently, while discussing the very poor fruits from her orchard last season, "We decided to pray instead of spray, and it didn't work." Spraying is just part of the general maintenance; not difficult, a bit of a bother at times, but worth it in the long run. Remember, an orchard is a permanent addition to your property, and one of nature's saddest scenes is the orchard that has been neglected. I don't know which bothers me most, the tree itself that looks like a forlorn, forgotten child or the fruit that hangs on its branches, withered and unusable.

We are all attracted by the ads for lawn and gardening equipment. Indeed, if we really went out and bought all the things we are told we need to maintain a small yard and a few trees, we'd have to build a large barn for storage. Men are little boys when it comes to tools and equipment, but I must say that all those bright shiny things are hard to resist. And it is true that to do a good job one must have good tools. (That's the best rationale for buying anything from a new typewriter to a trowel.) However, spraying equipment can be a bit scary if you don't know what you're getting into. We started out with a garden-hose-attachment-type sprayer. We have since graduated to the compressed air sprayer with a 2-gallon capacity. If you're big on power, there are sprayers that have a 10- to 30-gallon tank and are driven by small gasoline engines or electric motors. All of this will provide one or more happy Saturday mornings at your local hardware store and, in the long run, it's best to take their advice. Just buy this type of equipment from a reputable dealer so you have some recourse for service.

Housekeeping in the orchard is just as important as it is in your house. A poorly kept orchard is an open field for disease, insects and fungi. There is a spray schedule to follow for general use, but don't always treat by the calendar. Constant observation is the byword for orchard care. Know the physical condition of your trees as well as you know that of your cats and dogs. If you see something that doesn't look right—discolored, wilted leaves, scaly bark, dead twigs and branches—get advice from a professional. In this case, the professional is the agricultural experiment station. However, when it comes to answer-seeking, the professionals have a few requests they'd like to make.

First, the professionals warn us all not to expect perfection from our fruit trees. We are not going to get it. Therefore, we must decide for ourselves what is serious enough to worry about. Many times all the tree might need is a good washing with the hose. Secondly, these experts request that we learn to describe our problems clearly over the telephone. Obviously, they are not going to make house calls, and we can't go running to our nearest experiment station with a piece of the tree every time we suspect the worst. Usually a good clear verbal description is all that is necessary to get a prescription in return. This is not the way we handle our own ailments, but we're a bit more mobile than our fruit trees.

Following are some of the most prevalent problems to look for in your apple trees. These are generally found in areas where apples can be grown throughout the country.

APPLE SCAB: This ailment is easily recognized by olive-green spots on fruit and foliage. The spots grow and become velvety in appearance. You will start to see this in the spring and should start to control it early in the season.

RUST: Since rust is caused by fungi that complete part of their life cycle on the red cedar, it obviously does not make sense to plant your orchard near a stand of cedar trees. By sheer good luck we were spared this problem so common in New England and the Far West. Our cedar trees were so mangy looking that we cut them down without a qualm. Sometimes, however, you have to make a choice. If your trees have this condition, bright orange spots will appear on the leaves during rainy periods in early spring from green tip through petal fall (see Spray Schedule on page 39) .

POWDERY MILDEW: This problem is most common in New England and the Midwest. The fungus winters in the dormant buds, and the leaves will be covered with a white fungus growth.

FIREBLIGHT: Here is one of the more destructive diseases. It is most damaging during warm humid weather. The name is descriptive, as the stricken leaves and blossoms look as if they had been scorched. The best enemy of this disease is a dry, cool spring. Pruning, as well as spraying, is a good control. In late winter, cut and burn the infected twigs and branches.

APPLE MAGGOT: We have all seen this most destructive of insects. They are graphically named the railroad worms because of the brownish tracks they leave as they bore into the fruit. The fruit will have a bumpy appearance and the inside will be full of brown streaks. You can't even make applesauce out of these.

While it is necessary to be aware of the above problems, listing them in cold type can dampen enthusiasm for the potential orchardist. Actually there are certain things that can be done to control these diseases and pests in addition to spraying and they all come under the heading of "housekeeping." The following housekeeping tips apply to all fruit trees, not just apples.

- After the last fruits have been picked, remove all remaining fruits from the tree.
- Prune and remove all dead and diseased branches.
- Keep weeds and mulch away from the tree trunks.
- Make sure that the varieties you choose to grow are suited to your area.

Spraying is preventive medicine and it is a good idea to know just what you're up against from the beginning in the way of possible pests and diseases. As far as which sprays to use, it is best to check with your local experts on the subject as pesticides come and go on the market rapidly these days. Use a general-purpose spray that degrades soon after application.

If you have a tendency toward allergies, wear a mask over your face. In any case, spray on a clear and windless day and always follow directions on the package

GENERAL SPRAY SCHEDULE FOR APPLES

Dormant spray: Before the buds swell

Green tip: When green tissue first shows

Half-inch green: When ½ inch of green projects from buds

Tight cluster: When blossom buds are still tight; center bud may show some pink

Pink: When blossom buds are separate and all show pink but there are no open blossoms

Bloom: When 25% or more of buds are in bloom

Petal fall: When 80% of petals have fallen

First cover: One week after petal fall

Second cover: One week after first cover

Third cover: Two weeks after second cover

Fourth to eighth covers: Two-week intervals until early September

HARVESTING

Quite simply, the time to harvest is when the fruit tastes good. Try one and see. Hopefully you have kept a record of the varieties planted and know whether they are early, mid-season or late fruits so you can begin hovering around the orchard with your mouth watering at exactly the right moment. There are other signs of ripening in addition to the taste test. The skin of the apple will change in color from green to yellow or green to red, depending on the type. The skin will appear waxy. The seeds turn from white to brown. When you twist the apple it should come off the branch easily.

Store apples at a low temperature, near thirty-two degrees. The ideal place is in the refrigerator in plastic bags. Incidentally, did you know that a ripe apple gives off a gas that will hasten ripening of other fruits? Put one ripe apple in a bag with a pear, melon, banana or any other fruit. Leave the bag partially open to allow air to get in and let nature take its course.

VARIETIES

I cannot stress too strongly the importance of buying your trees from a reputable nursery. This will insure your starting off with healthy stock and, if the nursery is local, a lot of good advice will come with the trees. Also, the local grower will recommend varieties that may be peculiar to your geographic area, perhaps some new types that have just been put on the market for the home-grower. It's always fun to include a couple of new and different varieties.

The following are but a few of the hundreds of available varieties.

Baldwin: A crisp, juicy dessert apple that is also good for baking

Cortland: The one apple that does not turn brown after cutting. It's good for eating, salads, pies and sauces

Delicious: A good apple for eating

Earliblaze: An apple with good quality and flavor for eating and cooking

Empire: A fairly new, McIntosh-type, crisp apple for flavorful eating

Golden Delicious: Good for eating, sauces and pies

Golden Russet: A cider apple with high sugar content

Gravenstein: Good for eating and cooking

Jonathan: Good for eating and cooking; it's also a good keeper

Macoun: Excellent for eating

McIntosh: Good for eating and sauces

Monroe: Good for eating and cooking

Mutsu: A large, yellow Golden Delicious–type apple.

Northern Spy: Good for eating and pies

Prima: A new apple from Indiana; it is immune to apple scab

Rhode Island Greening: An early green apple for pies and sauces

Rome Beauty: The best baking apple

Spartan: A McIntosh-type apple, but firmer

Wealthy: An early apple; good for sauces and fried rings

Winesap: A late fall apple; good for eating and cooking

RECIPES

Apple Soup

4 TO 6 SERVINGS

1 tart, firm apple, unpeeled and quartered
1 medium onion, peeled and quartered
2 cans (13 ounces each) beef bouillon
Salt to taste
1 teaspoon curry powder or 1 tablespoon Scotch whiskey
1 pint medium or heavy cream

Place apple and onion in top of double boiler with bouillon. Put over simmering water and cook until apple and onion are soft and mushy. Strain into saucepan. Add salt to taste. When ready to serve, dissolve curry powder in small amount of cream and stir into soup. Add remaining cream and heat to the boiling point. Serve immediately. If using Scotch whiskey, stir in before heating.

Apple-Stuffed Veal Breast

6 SERVINGS

5 tablespoons butter
½ cup chopped onion
½ cup chopped celery
1 cup apple, peeled and diced
1½ cups soft breadcrumbs
½ teaspoon thyme
1 tablespoon chopped parsley
1 veal breast (3 to 4 pounds) with pocket
Flour for dredging
Salt to taste
Freshly ground pepper to taste
3 tablespoons apple brandy
½ cup chicken bouillon
½ cup cider
1 cup heavy cream
¼ cup minced parsley

Preheat oven to 325°. Heat 2 tablespoons butter in skillet and sauté onion and celery until soft. Stir in apple, breadcrumbs, thyme and parsley and toss all together. Fill pocket in veal breast with mixture and skewer opening. Season flour with salt and pepper, dredge meat in flour and brown in remaining butter on all sides. Warm apple brandy in small saucepan; pour over veal breast. Set veal aflame. When flame has died, place meat on rack in roasting pan and pour bouillon and cider into bottom of pan. Cover pan loosely with foil. Roast for 2 hours. Remove veal to warm serving platter. Pour pan juices into saucepan and set over high heat. Boil until slightly reduced. Add cream and bring to a boil. When thickened, pour over meat. Garnish with minced parsley.

Brandied Applesauce

3 CUPS

8 apples of different varieties
1 cup cider
1 cup dry white wine
1 cup confectioners' sugar
1 teaspoon cinnamon
½ teaspoon nutmeg
⅓ cup brandy

Put apples, unpeeled and uncored, into saucepan with cider and wine. Cover pan and place over medium heat. Let simmer until apples are soft and mushy. Put apples through food mill. Return to pan with liquid and add sugar, cinnamon and nutmeg. Cook over medium-low heat until sauce has thickened. Stir in brandy. Cook for 10 minutes longer. Serve warm with game, pork or poultry.

Apple Pockets

8 SERVINGS

1 cup butter
1 package (8 ounces) cream cheese, softened
2 cups flour
½ teaspoon salt
½ cup mixed dried fruit, chopped
¼ cup rum
2 large apples, peeled and cored
Rind of ½ orange, grated
¼ cup sugar
1 teaspoon cinnamon
¼ teaspoon nutmeg
1 egg yolk
1 tablespoon heavy cream

(continued)

43

Preheat oven to 375°. Mix together the butter and cream cheese until well blended. Mix in flour and salt to make a smooth dough. Roll into a ball, wrap in plastic wrap and chill for 1 hour.

Meanwhile, soak dried fruit in rum for 15 minutes.

Roll pastry out on floured board to $\frac{1}{4}$-inch thickness. Cut apples into eight $\frac{1}{2}$-inch-thick circles. Cut pastry into 16 circles $\frac{1}{2}$ inch larger than apple slices. Place each apple slice on a pastry circle and fill centers with dried fruit. Sprinkle with orange rind. Mix sugar, cinnamon and nutmeg together. Sprinkle mixture and remaining rum over apple slices. Cover with remaining pastry circles and press pastry edges together with a fork. Beat egg yolk, adding cream, and brush over circles.

Bake for 15 to 20 minutes until golden. Serve with vanilla ice cream sauce.

VANILLA ICE CREAM SAUCE

2 cups vanilla ice cream
1 egg
$\frac{1}{2}$ cup heavy cream
3 tablespoons rum

Soften ice cream and beat in egg. Whip cream very stiff and fold in. Stir in rum. Chill.

PEARS

Perhaps the most apt description of a pear is "food for the gods," which it was called many thousands of years ago when gods and goddesses ruled the world of man and beast. Mere mortals have used a wide variety of adjectives in an attempt to describe this beautiful fruit, from perfumed, fragrant and full-bodied to buttery, aromatic and fine-grained. It is certainly true that the flavor and virtue of a perfect pear are subtle and difficult to define. It must be juicy, it must be smooth, it must be mellow for eating; it must be crisp, slightly underripe and a bit gritty for cooking. A wise man once said, "One must sit up at night to eat a pear." We may take that to mean that there is an absolute moment of maturity at which a pear has reached perfection. Once that peak has passed it is a rapid slide downhill to deterioration.

Like its cousin the apple, the pear was with us from the beginning in these United States. The first pear tree was planted in Massachusetts in 1630. But unlike the apple, there are very few new varieties of pear; so we hang on to the old favorites for eating out of hand with a ripe Brie and a glass of white wine, for baking in a brandied coffee sauce, for combining with spices in a flavorful marmalade. It is unfortunate that "pear-shaped" is not regarded as a complimentary term, because the shape of a well-trimmed pear tree adorned with pale pink blossoms in the spring is a beautiful sight, as is the same tree bearing well-shaped fruit in the fall. The gods of old knew a good thing when they grew it.

SOIL

There is really not much to say about soil for pear trees that we haven't already said about apples. You want good garden soil, well drained. Pears can stand somewhat wetter feet than apples, so if you are planting on a hillside, the pears can go below the apples. They can take heavier loam (another word for soil) with a bit more clay in it. And, not that you can do much about it, pear trees like cool, moist, cloudy weather. This is good to know only if you have a particularly good crop one year and wonder why. Look back upon the weather.

PLANTING

If you are planting an orchard, as opposed to a bunch of fruit trees, then obviously you will have ordered several kinds and will put them in the ground at the same time. And when you dig, a hole is a hole is a hole. But one important consideration (and this does not apply to apples) is geographic location. Pears cannot take extreme temperatures and there is no point in planting them either far north or far south. They flower earlier than apples, so are more susceptible to winter chills.

Standard-sized pear trees must be planted at least 20 feet apart on all sides.

MULCHING

The rule for pear trees is *clean cultivation*—another phrase for your new orchard vocabulary. It simply means keeping the area around the trunk free of extraneous matter. The simplest way to do this is to cover the ground with clippings, chips or hay.

FERTILIZER

Because of fireblight—that dread disease that has made many people look upon this fruit as the hardest one to grow—you should fertilize the pear somewhat less than the apple. I've been told that keeping the amount of fertilizer down to $1/5$ pound per yearly age of the tree and no more than 4 pounds to a tree is a good idea.

PRUNING AND THINNING

It is variety, even in our hobbies, that makes life interesting, and don't think you can use just one set of rules for the whole orchard. The good news first: Pears require less pruning than other fruit trees. But, they do like "low heads." This means that the lowest branch should be no higher than 1½ feet from the ground. Why? Because the trunks suffer from fireblight, sunscald and winter injury and low branches protect the trunk. If you do see signs of the blight, cut off all affected limbs one foot into the healthy wood. Then burn these limbs some distance away from the tree.

Our main concern with the pear crop is thinning. Does the pear taste good? Larger pears have more flavor than smaller pears so you will have to courageously make the big sacrifice and thin out your fruits, eliminating the small pears. Soon after what is called the "June drop," pick the small fruit off the branches, leaving pears 6 inches apart. These will flourish and you will not be sorry when they come to a bountiful maturity.

POLLINATION

Here you may have a long discussion with your nursery man. It seems that there need be quite a bit of matchmaking done in the pear family to produce fruit. It is best to plant different varieties to insure pollination. You must also be sure to get types that will bloom simultaneously. You'd best ask the experts in your area for this advice.

INSECTS AND DISEASES

The spray schedule for pears is much the same as for apples. Thank goodness! Trying to spray individual trees would be a bit of a chore at best. In general, those insects that are attracted to the apple will also go for the pear. There is an insect peculiar to the pear called "Pear psylla." It shows up as a sticky substance on leaves and branches, but it can be controlled early in the game with the dormant spray.

HARVESTING

The moment has finally arrived, only it isn't a moment. It is a time of decision on your part and you may not make the right decision each time. Here again, keep a record and next year you'll be sure to do it right.

Different varieties of pears ripen at different times. Pears should be picked before they are fully ripe and ready to eat out of hand, but naturally you want the pear well developed so its flavor is full when you eat it. This sounds as if I'm begging the question and I am. If the green pear on the tree is turning slightly yellow and if, when you gently tip it up, the stem comes off the branch, it should be ready. Now it will finish its ripening process in your kitchen.

Be careful not to bruise the fruit when picking. Bruises become rotten spots, and there goes your pear. If you want to keep the pears for a while before eating, wrap them individually in soft paper and store them in a cool place. Bring them to an area with a temperature of seventy degrees to finish the ripening.

VARIETIES

If possible, choose your pears by the taste test. They are a fruit with very individual characteristics and they can be judged almost as one would judge a wine. Acid content, sweetness, aroma and general character of flavor are all important with this subtle fruit. Plant what you like to eat.

Bartlett: The most commonly used pear for eating out of hand and canning

Beurre Bosc: A cinnamon-colored, aromatic and juicy pear

Beurre d'Anjou: A good keeper. A late, large fruit with dull, yellow skin

Clapp's Favorite: A late summer pear. It is large and flavorful and not a good keeper

Comice: A beautiful pear that is sweet and highly perfumed

Flemish Beauty: A rich, honey-flavored pear

Kieffer: A pear for southern orchards. It is large, yellow-skinned and good for preserves, but it is too grainy for eating

Moonglow: A vigorous tree; late bloomer

Seckel: Small and brownish; sweet and spicy for cooking. A must for home orchards. It is a hardy and healthy tree, bearing small fruit. Considered by many to be the best in quality and richness of flavor

Starlang Delicious: An excellent quality fruit

RECIPES

Baked Stuffed Pears

4 SERVINGS

> 4 winter pears
> Approximately ¼ cup chopped dates
> Approximately ¼ cup chopped nuts
> 1 cup brown sugar
> ½ cup water
> ½ teaspoon cinnamon
> ¼ teaspoon ginger
> 1 tablespoon grated lemon rind

Preheat oven to 300°. With vegetable peeler remove cores of pears, making a hollow down the middle of the whole fruit. Mix together dates and nuts. Fill space in pears with the date-and-nut mixture. Stand the pears up in a deep casserole or bean pot large enough to hold pears side by side. Combine the sugar, water, cinnamon, ginger and lemon rind and heat in saucepan until sugar is dissolved. Pour over pears. Cover and bake for 1 to 1½ hours until pears are tender but still have their shape. Serve warm with cream.

Pear-Glazed Pork Loin

4 TO 5 SERVINGS

> 1 pork loin roast (4 pounds)
> Salt to taste
> Freshly ground black pepper to taste
> ½ cup pear and ginger marmalade (see below)
> ¼ cup frozen orange juice concentrate
> 2 tablespoons soy sauce
> 1 small clove garlic
> 1 tablespoon lemon juice
> 1½ cups pears, peeled and sliced (about 2 pears)

Preheat oven to 325°. Place pork roast on rack in roasting pan and sprinkle with salt and pepper. Roast for 1 hour.

Meanwhile, put marmalade, orange juice, soy sauce, garlic and lemon juice in blender and puree. Spoon half of mixture over roast at end of 1 hour of roasting. Roast 20 minutes longer. Cover with remaining mixture and roast another 20 minutes. Add pears to pan 10 minutes before removing from oven.

Pear and Ginger Marmalade

ABOUT 6 JARS (8 OUNCES EACH)

> 6 cups sugar
> Juice of 2 lemons
> Rind of 2 lemons, grated
> 10 cups pears, slightly underripe and sliced (about 12 pears)
> ¼ cup preserved or crystalized ginger

Combine sugar, lemon rind and juice. Place pears in large saucepan in alternate layers with sugar-lemon mixture. Let stand 2 or 3 hours. Add ginger. Bring to a boil. Allow to boil, uncovered, stirring frequently until thick and clear, about 45 minutes. Pour into sterilized jars, cool slightly and seal, following the Instructions for Preserving on page 185.

Pear Tart

Pastry for one 8-inch crust, pre-baked for 10 minutes at
    425°
1 tablespoon apricot jam
1 teaspoon brandy
2 tablespoons finely ground almonds
4 cups pears, peeled and sliced (about 5 pears)
½ cup sugar
2 tablespoons lemon juice
½ cup brown sugar
½ cup flour
⅓ cup butter
½ teaspoon cinnamon
½ teaspoon nutmeg
¼ teaspoon ginger

Preheat oven to 400°. Heat apricot jam and thin with brandy. Brush pie shell with jam and sprinkle with almonds. Toss pears with sugar and lemon juice and place in pie shell. Mix together the remaining 6 ingredients until crumbly. Cover pears with mixture. Bake for 45 minutes till golden.

PEACHES

The poet's "rosy blush" of the perfect peach is the grower's sign that it is ripe and ready for eating. How you choose to eat it is up to you. You may follow the example of the young gentleman who stood under the ripest peaches on the tree, hands behind his back, and ate large bites of the fruit while the juices ran down his chin or the elderly lady who cautiously covered her lap with a large damask napkin, sliced the peach in half with a knife and ate the fruit out of the skin with a silver teaspoon.

I prefer the elderly lady's method, especially for the white-fleshed Belle of Georgia whose delicate flavor should not be overwhelmed with any other perfumes. This is an early ripening peach; later you will have the golden varieties—some with the familiar names of Hale Haven, Sunqueen and Elberta. Others, perhaps not so familiar, are the Richaven, a new variety with clear yellow flesh that resists browning, Red Haven, which has an almost perfectly smooth skin and the old-fashioned Crawford, with its many-shaded red flesh and rich flavor.

You see, a peach is not just a peach; it comes in many varieties to suit a variety of needs. The pie lover may choose one kind, the chutney maker another. The amateur orchardist may have difficulty making a choice. Here again, the nursery catalogs will be very helpful. Just be sure to pick your peach trees with their ripening times uppermost in your mind. It is better to plan so that your crop spreads out over a six- to eight-week period than it is to be overwhelmed with ripe fruit all at once, having to eat more than your share of puddings, pies and cakes with the preserving kettle steaming for twelve hours a day. A lot of good fruit is lost this way.

SOIL

Since the peach speaks best with a southern accent, its natural tendencies are toward warmth and sun. In a word, it grows best in the South, and like many southern ladies it thrives on attention. However, with the proper amount of tender loving care it can be made to grow and produce very well in most of the other states with the exception of areas where there may be sustained temperatures below zero degrees. For instance, Minnesota, Wisconsin and the Dakotas are not good locations for peach trees so forget it and concentrate on something else. You can always buy the fruit in season and there's enough struggle in growing without taking on a project that has all of the odds against it.

The soil has a definite influence on the hardiness of this tree. Naturally, it likes soil that is warm and dry so it's up to us to provide a condition that will hold heat for the roots. This would mean the addition of sand, gravel or even stones. If you've ever cooked at a beach, you know how all of these properties hold warmth for a long time.

Peaches will grow in a wide variety of soils provided they are not too rich. Rich soil produces lush foliage, but less fruit, and, in the northern states, the wood does not mature, bringing on possible winter injury. The necessary pH? Between 6.0 and 6.5.

PLANTING

The need for good drainage goes without saying and, ideally, if you just happen to have a gentle slope that is near water with a bit of shelter, such as slight hills and woods, then quickly plant peach trees. They'll love it. Plant them 18 feet apart and avoid low frost pockets. As heat rises, cold air runs downhill.

MULCHING

Peach trees do not grow well in sod. They like a clean area around the trunk with a small amount of mulch. Spread the mulch a bit away from the trunk, as it can breed insects that would go for the wood.

FERTILIZING

As with other fruit trees, nitrogen is the important word.

Peaches take ¼ to ½ pound per year of age. Spread it over the ground so the snows and winter rains will take it into the root system.

PRUNING AND THINNING

Your peach trees will keep you busy with the pruning shears. They need it and for a very good reason. (It always helps to know *why*.) Both the peach and the nectarine bear fruit from lateral buds on year-old twigs. In order to produce a good crop of fruit each year it is necessary to continuously stimulate new growth.

The peach should be a low-head tree with an open center. That should be easy to visualize. Again there is a very good reason for this. If the tree were to grow high it would be wide open to wind damage, and certainly it is easier to prune, thin and harvest this way.

You really want three scaffolds (main limbs) on the peach tree. At planting time cut the main scaffold down to 24 inches. If there are two adjoining branches that are large and pretty much the same size, cut to 10 inches and leave them. If they are weak and spindly, cut them to stubs, 1 to 2 inches, and pick out two good scaffolds the following spring. The three scaffolds should form wide angles with the trunk, nice and open. There should be no sharp corners or they will split off. They also should be distributed evenly around the trunk. Each spring you must remove the excess branches and suckers coming up from the roots and any extraneous growth that looks untidy.

Believe it or not, this is really not much pruning compared to what you're going to do when the peach trees get older. Then they will need severe trimming to maintain and renew their growth because with slower growth they become less vigorous, as do we all.

There is no hard and fast, right or wrong, way to prune. If you start out training the tree properly, you will get to know its personality and work from there. This is one of the nice things about a small orchard. Each tree is an individual and can be treated that way. Large commercial orchards are a different matter but that is big business.

Thinning peach trees is important too. This hurts, especially when in some areas the tree sets two to five times more fruit than should be allowed to mature. However, this seemingly drastic measure is necessary to achieve larger fruit and destroy insects and fungi. About a month after the fruits are set, go out and pick off enough to leave fruit 4 to 5 inches apart. You won't feel badly later when you serve a bowl of perfectly poached peaches, their golden flesh tinged with the "rosy blush," bathed in a winy syrup.

POLLINATION

Most peach trees are self-fruitful, but who wants just one of any fruit tree? If you only have room for two, plant one white-fleshed and one yellow-fleshed.

INSECTS AND DISEASES

Peaches have some of the same diseases and insects that other fruit trees have with a couple that are especially their own. If you do not spray, you will probably be cursed with peach leaf curl, which can make a mess of your trees. The leaves curl inward, are blistered and distorted and drop off—an ugly sight. Another problem is the peach tree borer, which attacks the trunk and branches. You can't miss the symptoms if you are really looking at your trees. There is also the San Jose scale and scab to worry about. So spray you must, although not quite as often as for pears and apples.

GENERAL SPRAY SCHEDULE FOR PEACHES

Dormant spray: Early spring before buds swell
Pink: Just before blooms open
Bloom: When 90% of blossoms are open

Petal fall: When last petals are falling
First cover: One week after petal fall
Second cover: Two weeks after first cover
Third cover: Two weeks after second cover
Remaining covers: Spray every two weeks to within two weeks
of harvest

HARVESTING

Like the employer who tells the college graduate applying for
his first job, "You must have experience," the experts say that
experience will tell you when to harvest your peach crop. But
there must be some guidelines the first year around. There are.

Test the peach on the tree as you have been testing them in
the market up to now. A little pressure with the fingers and if
the flesh gives a bit, it is ready. Another test is color. When the
skin of the white-fleshed peach turns from greenish to yellow
and the yellow-fleshed peach turns from yellowish to orange, the
fruit is ripe. Never give the peach a direct pull; just twist gently.
This fruit bruises easily. Believe it or not, it is claimed that
women are better peach pickers than men—less awkward. In our
family there is no discrimination when picking time comes. We
need all hands, male and female. Peaches ripen best in the
refrigerator. When you want to eat them, bring them to room
temperature and use them soon.

VARIETIES

Here it is very important to get the advice of a local grower.
There is a condition called "delayed foliation" that occurs with
these trees. This means that in the spring they will flower and
leaf out erratically if they have not had a long enough period of
dormancy under chilling conditions. This used to present a
great problem in the southern California type of climate, but
now varieties have been developed to cope with the warm winters in some states.

There are hundreds of varieties of peaches, with new ones
being developed all the time. I would advise planting both the

white and yellow freestone, called poetically the "yellow melt-ing-flesh." Surely, that is a perfect description of the peach we would all like to grow.

RECIPES

Peach Tart

SWEET PASTRY

½ cup butter
1 cup flour
3 tablespoons confectioners' sugar

Preheat oven to 425°. Place all ingredients in bowl. Mix to-gether with fingers into a crumbly dough. Place in 8-inch tart pan and, with heel of hand, push into place, making sure dough goes well up sides of pan. Prick bottom with fork. Place in freezer for 1 hour.

Bake tart shell for 12 minutes until just browned.

FILLING

4 cups peaches, peeled and sliced (about 5 peaches)
½ cup brown sugar
¼ cup granulated sugar
½ teaspoon cinnamon
3 egg yolks
⅔ cup heavy cream

Preheat oven to 400°. Arrange sliced peaches in tart shell. Sprinkle with sugars and cinnamon. Bake for 15 minutes. Turn heat down to 375°. Beat egg yolks, adding cream. Pour over peaches and bake for 30 minutes until filling is set. Cool before cutting.

Rum Peach Marmalade

4 TO 5 JARS (8 OUNCES EACH)

1 orange
5 cups peaches, peeled and sliced (about 4 peaches)
2 tablespoons lemon juice
6 cups sugar
½ cup amber rum

Remove peel, white pith and seeds from orange. Chop or grind peel and flesh of orange. Put peaches, orange, lemon juice and sugar into large saucepan. Boil, stirring frequently, until mixture thickens. This will take 45 to 60 minutes, depending upon condition of fruit. Ladle into sterilized jars, following the Instructions for Preserving on page 185. Add 2 tablespoons rum to each jar. Seal.

Honeyed Peaches

Peaches
Honey
Brandy

Dip peaches in rapidly boiling water for a count of ten. Remove and slip off skins. Mix equal parts of honey and brandy and roll fruit in this mixture, covering the peaches all over. Place in bowl. Cover tightly with plastic wrap. Refrigerate. Serve icy cold.

Brandied Peaches

8 JARS (32 OUNCES EACH)

Approximately 3 dozen peaches
1 lemon, sliced
4 cups brown sugar
1 navel orange, sliced
2 cups white sugar
3 tablespoons whole cloves
4 cups cider vinegar
4 cinnamon sticks
2 cups cider
2 cups brandy

Scald and peel peaches. Put the remaining ingredients except the brandy into a large saucepan. Boil until syrup is clear. Add peaches, a few at a time, and cook uncovered about 10 minutes. Put into sterilized jars, following the Instructions for Preserving on page 185. Pour 2 ounces brandy into each jar. Boil syrup down until slightly thickened and fill jars. Seal. Leftover syrup may be refrigerated and used for other fruits.

After peaches have been opened, save syrup for other uses, such as thinning pancake batter, flavoring drinks and mincemeat, stirring into custards and sauces.

CHERRIES

Housman's "loveliest of trees" has been used by writers down through the ages to express beauty, faith, love and, as every red-blooded American boy knows too well, truth ("George . . . who killed that beautiful little cherry tree yonder in the garden?"). While we never do find out which variety of cherry he is referring to, it was most likely a sweet cherry, possibly the Morello, as the sour cherry does not grow well south of the Potomac; and we may be sure that the pie baked for "Billy-boy" was made of the tart cherry, probably that old faithful, Montmorency.

In any case and in any climate, it makes sense to have cherry trees in your orchard. They are the easiest of all stone fruits to grow, and where else will you get cherries for that pie, those tarts, the *kuchen* and the brandied cherry preserves?

It is good for the orchardist's morale to have a fruit tree that bears early and abundantly. As one Victorian authoress rhapsodized, "The entire tree drips with its pendulous globules of luscious fruitage." Somehow she does not mind combining this airy prose with a recipe for the heaviest of steamed puddings. However, her meaning is clear and I can personally attest to the fruitage. With just two sour and one sweet we have had all the cherries we could use in one season.

SOIL

Sour cherries prefer the same climate that apples do. They like it cold with a high chilling factor, and they like the same type of well-drained, deep loam or clay. Incidentally, of the two, the sour cherries are the easier to grow. The sweet cherry is like the peach in temperament and prefers a dry, gravelly or sandy soil. I must add that our three cherry trees are growing right next to each other and seem to be happy in their element. These variables, which are present in any type of gardening, make us realize that there are no hard and fast rules—only guidelines.

PLANTING

Plant your sour cherries 18 feet apart and the sweet cherries 20 to 22 feet apart. In a cold climate do the planting in the spring; in a warm climate plant in the fall.

MULCHING

These trees should be well mulched and cultivation around them is important. This means keeping the soil loose and friable and not hard and packed down. As we go on with this orchard, it becomes apparent that the best thing for the health of your fruit trees is to have as little sod as possible around them. For years my husband tried to talk me into just forgetting about lawn and covering the ground in the orchard with hay. My esthetic sense said no, but he has finally won his battle. Perhaps I should say the trees have won theirs because I am convinced that they are much happier and healthier without the sod around them to take away the nutrients. It really doesn't look too bad either. As a gardening friend once observed, a lawn is a totally non-productive worry, and it is expensive to maintain besides.

FERTILIZING

Beyond the fertilizing that you may do when you first plant, these trees do not need much. Unless you notice signs of general disability, they can do very well on what is naturally in the soil, fed by the mulch.

PRUNING

The trees supplied by your nursery will probably be two-year-old grafted trees. That is, they are two years old from the time of grafting. In this case they will be fairly well branched. Leave 4 to 5 branches on the main stem and trim them shorter than the leader (trunk). The lowest branch should be 15 to 20 inches above the ground, and the branches around the tree should be well spaced. Basically, you want to prune for easy picking, so leave an open center. The sour cherry tends to be the more brittle of the two, so make sure its branches are at wide angles to the trunk. The sweet cherry will grow taller and straighter; just let it do as it wishes, trimming out the dead and injured branches.

POLLINATION

Here we have a rather complicated picture and there is no point in your trying to memorize which varieties can pollinate other varieties. You'd better get advice from a professional on which trees to plant. The best advice is to never plant just one tree of any one variety.

INSECTS AND DISEASES

The sour cherry is easier to maintain for one big reason: It is more disease resistant. It can contract brown rot and various fungi and blights, but they can all be controlled by spraying. "Black-knot," a disease also found on the plum, is controlled by cutting out the diseased parts of the tree.

The cherry tree has its share of attacking insects, although fewer than do other trees in the orchard. Most of these insects are also found on peaches and plums. There is one, however, that reminds us of that old saying, "What is worse than finding a worm in an apple?" The cherry has something called a "cherry fruit maggot," which is a small, whitish worm that can end up in the cherry pie if you don't get after it in the early stages. The "plum curculio" also likes cherries and should be eliminated.

GENERAL SPRAY SCHEDULE FOR CHERRIES

Prebloom: Just before first blossoms open
Bloom: When most blossoms are open
Petal fall: When most petals have fallen
Shuck fall: When shucks begin to fall from fruit

Ten days after shuck fall, when fruit begins to color, no more spray is needed.

HARVESTING

Whenever the subject of growing our own cherries comes up, someone invariably asks, "What about the birds?" There is always the answer, "Plant enough for the birds too," but in a small backyard operation that will not work—so we must find other ways to selfishly keep our cherry crop for ourselves. Netting is one answer, but it is a lot of trouble on large trees. The other is a very simple solution that was developed in California and has instant appeal because of its very simple, and somewhat whimsical, side. Take a spool of black *cotton* thread and throw it back and forth across the tree, creating a web of thread. The birds will not enter this web for fear of entangling their wings and, if the thread is cotton, it will dissolve by itself after the season is over. Yes, it works.

When it comes to picking, I find it easier to pick without the stems and usually this will leave the pits behind also. Pitting cherries seems to be an individualistic thing. I prefer an old-fashioned pitter, my husband prefers a sharp knife and the children apparently prefer not to pit at all. We discovered this after eating a nonpitted cherry pie one evening.

Cherries do not keep well in the refrigerator—they develop brown spots where the pits have been removed—but they do freeze very well. Measure them by cupfuls and add the necessary amount of sugar for a pie. Spoon them into labeled plastic containers and then put the containers in the freezer. Four cups of cherries mixed with one cup of sugar will make a 9-inch pie.

VARIETIES

Cherries are grown on two stocks—Mazzard and Mahaleb. The Mazzard is really the wild sweet cherry and is by far the better stock. The trees grow bigger, live longer and give a more abundant crop. As the Mahaleb is the easier one to find, you may have to do a bit of research to get hold of the Mazzard. With cherry trees, it would be best to consult your local nursery or agriculture experiment station as to which will produce best in your area; also find out how to handle the pollination problems. In addition to the sweet and sour there is another variety called "Duke." This is a hybrid between the other two and requires cross-pollination with either a sweet or a sour.

RECIPES

Sour Cherry Cake

½ cup butter or margarine
1½ cups sugar
3 eggs
3 cups flour
2 teaspoons baking powder
½ teaspoon baking soda
1 teaspoon cinnamon
½ teaspoon allspice
½ teaspoon ground cloves
¼ teaspoon salt
1 cup milk
2 cups sour cherries, pitted (about 1 pound cherries)
Kirsch to taste
Almonds, toasted, to garnish

Preheat oven to 350°. Cream together the butter and sugar until smooth and light. Beat in eggs, one at a time. In another bowl, mix together the flour, baking powder, baking soda and spices. Beat flour mixture and milk alternately into the butter mixture. Stir in the cherries. Turn batter into two greased and floured 9-inch cake tins. Bake for 30 minutes. Let rest at room temperature for 10 minutes. Turn out onto racks to cool. Frost with a butter-sugar icing flavored with kirsch to taste. Sprinkle top with toasted almonds.

4 tablespoons heavy cream
4 tablespoons butter
2 cups confectioners' sugar

Beat all ingredients together till smooth.

Black Cherry Mold

6 SERVINGS

1 envelope unflavored gelatin
1 cup grape juice
1 cup sherry
½ cup Bourbon whiskey
2 cups black cherries, pitted (about 1 pound cherries)

Add gelatin to ¼ cup grape juice and stir till dissolved. Heat remaining grape juice in small saucepan and add gelatin-grape mixture. Stir over low heat till gelatin has melted. Stir in sherry and Bourbon. Fold in cherries and turn into a 5- to 6-cup mold—a ring mold will do. Chill several hours until firm. Turn out and serve with a custard sauce flavored with Bourbon.

CUSTARD SAUCE

2 cups milk
3 egg yolks
½ cup sugar
Bourbon whiskey to taste

Scald milk in saucepan. In bowl, beat yolks and sugar until blended. Beat in hot milk. Return mixture to saucepan and stir over medium heat until thickened. Do not boil. Cool. Flavor with Bourbon to taste.

Spiced Cherry Sauce

ABOUT 3 CUPS

1 jar (8 ounces) currant jelly
¼ cup Port wine
1 cinnamon stick, 1 inch long
2 cups black cherries, pitted and halved (about 1 pound cherries)
1 tablespoon grated lemon rind
1 tablespoon grated orange rind

Put jelly, wine and cinnamon stick in small saucepan and heat together uncovered over medium heat until syrupy, about 10 minutes. Stir in cherries and fruit rinds. Simmer uncovered for 10 minutes. Remove cinnamon stick. Pour sauce into glass, plastic or china container and refrigerate until ready to use. Serve at room temperature with lamb or pork. Excellent with grilled meats.

PLUMS

The name "prunus domesticus" certainly does not reveal the diverse personalities of the common garden plum. It sounds so dull and mundane with no suggestion of its wonderful range of colors, flavors and aromas. We do get a hint of the possibilities of plums when we think of Jack Horner, who apparently pulled out the best plum of all; and the old "visions of sugar plums" makes us wish for the sweetest of sweets, although they were probably prunes that had been rolled in sugar and dried.

Certainly the plum has a wider color range than any of our orchard fruits, going from green and yellow through red and purple to almost black; and with today's convenient shipping from coast to coast we may encounter these fruits in our markets during their harvest season. But as a well-known food writer said about modern marketing, "What we gain in convenience we lose in anticipation."

There are hundreds of varieties of plums that can be grown in the home orchard with comparatively little trouble. Some plums are better when cooked for jams, sauces, cakes and tarts. Others are best when eaten ripe from the tree, when they are at their height of rich flavor and perfume. And don't forget the prune, that by-product of the sweetest plum that makes a pork roast something special on the menu. Poached plums with cinnamon-touched whipped cream, brandied plum cakes and greengage plum ice cream . . . surely we could make good culinary use of this versatile fruit if we picked it from our own trees. A good crop is a challenge, and if we grow it we will not waste it.

Happily, plums of one sort or another will grow in any part of the country so there is no reason to exclude them from your orchard plan, unless, of course, you don't like them. There is no substitute for the taste test, so go around and sample different kinds; some will definitely appeal to you more than others and those are the ones you should plant. Bear in mind, though, that if you live in northern Wisconsin and were captivated by a plum you ate in southern California, there is no way to bring the two together. The common garden plum is poorly named; it is far from being a dull fruit.

SOIL

As with the cherry, we are talking here about two different types of tree and, therefore, two different types of soil. The Japanese plum is like the peach in that both are sensitive to cold and prefer a warmer climate and soil. The European plum generally seems to be the best for the United States, and does not mind if its soil is heavy.

PLANTING

As there is a type of plum suitable for just about every climate in the country, it is not hard to find one to suit your needs. However, plum trees do need to be winter chilled in order to bear fruit. The temperature should go below forty degrees for a few weeks, but not below twenty-five degrees for any prolonged length of time. Avoid low-lying frost pockets as they will endanger early bloom.

Plant in the fall if you have mild winters; otherwise plant in the spring while the trees are still dormant. Space plum trees from 20 to 25 feet apart and cut back the growth on a new tree by 25%. Plum trees are especially sensitive to sunscald (sunburn to you), so you might consider wrapping the lower part of the tree in burlap to prevent this.

MULCHING

The needs of the plum with respect to mulching are the same as those of the peach. They need a small amount of mulch spread away from the trunk.

FERTILIZING

Fertilizing requirements for plum trees are so much like peach requirements that it is not necessary to repeat the details. Just think peach and plum together, as in a pie of the same name, and it will all work out right.

PRUNING

By this time, you are so adept with the pruning shears and so familiar with the language of pruning that if I mention "open center" or "central leader," you won't have to think twice. (See page 70 in case you do.) Just make sure you know which tree is which. The European varieties (Greengage, Bradshaw, Prune) take to the central leader pruning; the Japanese (Santa Rosa, Burbank, Formosa) like the open or vase shape, which can be achieved by pruning out the central leader.

Basically, you want a well-shaped, strong tree that is capable of supporting heavy crops and withstanding strong winds. Here again, you should think about the tree and its purpose, which is to bear the most and best fruit it can. If the fruit is well distributed around the tree and has an abundance of light and air it should respond well. Plums do lean toward a confusion of branches with many overlaps and crisscrosses; therefore, they need a lot of pruning as they mature to keep them under control. Why the difference in pruning the two varieties? It is because of the different bearing habits of the two. The Japanese plum tree mostly bears fruit on twigs and spurs of new wood. The European plum bears its fruits on spurs of old wood.

POLLINATION

As most plums are self-sterile you will need at least two varieties.

INSECTS AND DISEASES

Spray the plum the same way you spray its closest friend and neighbor, the peach, who very kindly gives it one of its own worst enemies, the peach borer. The plum also faces something

OPEN CENTER
PRUNING

CENTRAL
LEADER
PRUNING

called the "plum curculio," which is another insect. Its most troublesome diseases are brown rot and black-knot. For these, you must prune out the damaged limbs and destroy them immediately. Also destroy all "mummied" fruit. (I'm sure you can figure out what those look like.)

If you live in an area that still has fields, meadows or woods around it, besides being very lucky to have open space in this day and age, you may also have wild fruit trees growing near you. These trees have not been taken care of, produce no fruit and could harbor the very insects and diseases that you are trying so hard to control. My advice would be to cut them down. Fruitwood is lovely for furniture and boat models.

HARVESTING

Plums for eating out of hand must be dead ripe when picked because their flavor develops while still hanging. They are ready when they have a springy softness and are sweet to the taste. They keep quite well—a week or so in a cool place—and, as they tend to ripen in stages, you should not be deluged with fruit.

VARIETIES

There are literally hundreds of varieties of this so-called "cosmopolitan" fruit. We tend to lean toward the names we know, so you would do just as well to ask a local authority which do best in your area. The only difficulty you should have with plums is in limiting your choice to the few you have space for in the orchard.

RECIPES

Baked Sugar Plums

6 SERVINGS

12 large plums, halved and stoned (about 2 pounds plums)
1/2 cup sugar
1/2 cup coarsely chopped walnuts
2 to 3 tablespoons sherry

Preheat oven to 325°. Place plum halves in flat baking dish, cut side up. Sprinkle with sugar, walnuts and sherry. Bake for 15 to 20 minutes until plums are glazed. Serve warm with sour cream for dessert.

Plum Brûlée

Sweet pastry for one 8-inch piecrust (see page 57)
8 to 12 plums, halved and stoned (1½ to 2 pounds plums)
1 package (3 ounces) cream cheese, softened
1 cup whipping cream
1/4 cup very fine sugar
1 tablespoon lemon juice
1/2 teaspoon cinnamon
1/2 cup brown sugar

Preheat oven to 425°. Fit tart pastry into 8-inch pie or tart pan. Put in freezer for 1 hour. Bake tart shell for 15 to 20 minutes until a golden brown. Let cool.

Arrange plums close together on bottom of tart shell. With

mixer, beat cream cheese until soft. Beat in cream gradually. Beat in sugar, lemon juice and cinnamon. Spoon over plums. Chill for about 2 hours until firm. Sieve brown sugar evenly over top of tart, covering filling completely. Broil about 3 inches below heat until sugar begins to caramelize. This will only take a minute, so watch carefully. Let cool.

Poached Plums

6 red plums, halved and pitted (about 1 pound plums)
6 purple plums, halved and pitted (about 1 pound plums)
1 cup sugar
3 tablespoons rum
4 tablespoons orange juice
2 tablespoons crystalized ginger

Place plums in large saucepan. Add sugar, rum and orange juice. Bring to a boil and simmer, covered, for 10 to 15 minutes until plums are just tender. With a slotted spoon, remove plums to serving dish. Boil syrup down until slightly thickened. Pour over plums. Sprinkle with finely chopped crystalized ginger. Chill and serve with cream.

Prune Pecan Cake

1¼ cups butter or margarine
2½ cups sugar
5 eggs
1½ teaspoons baking powder
3¼ cups flour
1 cup chopped packaged prunes
1 cup chopped pecans
½ teaspoon salt
⅔ cup buttermilk

(continued)

Preheat oven to 350°. Cream butter and sugar until light and creamy. Beat in eggs, one at a time. In another bowl, mix baking powder with 1/4 cup of flour and set aside. Mix prunes and pecans with 1/2 cup of flour in another bowl and set aside. Mix salt with remaining flour in a fourth bowl. Add flour-salt mixture and buttermilk alternately to creamed butter-sugar-egg mixture, blending well. Stir in baking powder–flour mixture. Fold in prune-nut-flour mixture.

Turn into a greased and floured 10-inch tube pan. Bake for 1 hour and 20 minutes or until cake tests done. Let cool in pan for 10 minutes. Run a knife around the edge and turn out onto rack. Tip cake back into pan and sprinkle with rum-butter sauce. Leave cake in pan for 10 minutes. Invert onto plate and let cool before slicing.

RUM-BUTTER SAUCE

2 tablespoons butter
1/4 cup dark or amber rum
1 cup sugar
1/3 cup water

Put butter, rum and sugar into small saucepan. Bring to a boil, stirring. When butter has melted, add water. Cook for 5 minutes. While hot, pour onto cake.

APRICOTS

One must be an apricot devotee to plant this lovely fruit tree because it is not generally included in the orchard plan. If you have room, and appreciate the possibilities of this delicate amber-hued fruit, by all means plant an apricot tree.

Moongold and Sungold are two of the most popular varieties and their names alone should tempt you, without even tasting a cold apricot cream, rich apricot pudding or an unusual chicken baked with apricot halves.

Apricots are self-fruitful so there is no need to plant more than one unless, as with other trees of this type, you wish to be on the safe side. They are included with the peach for general planting, pruning and cultivation care. As a matter of fact, the apricot gets short shrift in many books with the words "plant a peach instead; its care and uses are about the same." Not so, if you really know your fruits. Perhaps the canned varieties taste much the same, but not the fresh ones from the tree. You might even try drying your own apricots if you have a large enough crop. You would be amazed at how different they are from the commercial variety. I think one of the nicest presents I ever received was a large box of apricots that had been picked from a friend's tree in California, dried and rushed via airmail to me in Connecticut. I cherished and savored every one and decided right then that someday I would have my own apricot tree.

RECIPES

Game Hens with Glazed Apricots

4 SERVINGS

4 large Cornish game hens, split
Salt to taste
Freshly ground pepper to taste
½ teaspoon thyme
4 tablespoons butter
1 tablespoon oil
½ cup chicken bouillon
2 shallots, chopped
8 apricots, pitted and halved (about 1 pound apricots)
2 tablespoons lemon juice
½ cup dry white wine
¼ cup sugar

Preheat oven to 350°. Sprinkle birds with salt, pepper and thyme. Heat 2 tablespoons of butter and the 1 tablespoon of oil in a large skillet. Brown birds on all sides. Remove to baking dish large enough to hold birds in one layer. Pour in bouillon. Cover dish and put in oven. Bake for 20 minutes.

Add remaining butter to skillet and sauté shallots until soft. Add apricot halves and sauté until glazed. Spoon apricot halves and shallots into baking dish with game hens. Add lemon juice, white wine and sugar to skillet and bring to a boil. Pour over game hens. Cover and bake for another 20 minutes. Serve with a rice pilaf.

Anne's Apricot Cake

2 tablespoons butter
½ cup brown sugar
12 large apricots, pitted and halved (1½ to 2 pounds apricots)
½ cup butter
½ cup sugar
1 egg
½ teaspoon baking soda
½ cup plain yogurt
1 cup flour
1½ teaspoons baking powder
¼ teaspoon almond extract
2 tablespoons brandy

Preheat oven to 375°. Put 2 tablespoons butter into a 6 x 8½ x 2-inch baking dish (or any shallow oblong dish). Place dish in oven and heat until butter is melted. Sprinkle brown sugar over bottom of dish. Arrange apricot halves over sugar. Cream together the ½ cup butter and sugar until smooth. Beat in egg. Add soda to yogurt. Add baking powder to flour. Beat yogurt and flour mixtures alternately into butter mixture. When smooth, blend in almond extract and brandy. Pour into prepared baking dish. Bake for 30 minutes until cake tests done. Serve warm with brandied whipped cream.

BRANDIED WHIPPED CREAM

1 cup heavy whipping cream
½ cup sugar
2 tablespoons brandy

Whip cream until stiff, adding sugar and brandy.

Stuffed Apricots

12 apricots (about 1½ pounds apricots)
¼ cup butter
¼ cup maple syrup
1 cup corn or whole wheat breadcrumbs
Grated rind of 1 orange

Preheat oven to 325°. Leave apricots unpeeled or, if you prefer, scald and skin them quickly. Slit open a bit on one side and remove pit. Heat butter with syrup and stir in breadcrumbs and orange rind. Stuff whole apricots with this mixture. Place in oven-proof dish and heat for 15 minutes. Serve as a garnish to ham, pork or duck.

Frozen Apricot Cream

8 SERVINGS

8 to 10 apricots (about 1 pound apricots)
2 tablespoons lemon juice
1 cup sugar
½ can condensed milk
1 cup heavy cream

Scald and peel apricots. Remove pits. Puree apricots in blender with lemon juice. Stir in sugar and milk. In a small bowl, whip cream until stiff. Combine apricots with cream and fill a 5-cup mold. Cover mold tightly and freeze for several hours. Unmold onto platter and garnish with apricot halves and frosted grapes.

....
....

CHAPTER 2

DWARF FRUIT TREES

If you've gotten this far in the book and are saying to yourself, "Thanks for the recipes, but if I have to allow 20 feet for each tree I'd better buy my fruit at the market," don't give up. There is a solution for those of us who don't have land area for the standard-sized fruit trees.

The British know what it is to garden in small spaces; on an island there is no room for expansion. Perhaps that is why they were the ones to research and develop a series of rootstocks for dwarf apple trees. Malling IX is the most widely used and the most dwarfing of the rootstocks developed at the East Malling Research Station at Kent, England. This tree usually grows no higher than 8 feet. Since it all started with the apple (many important things have) there is a much wider selection of varieties in that fruit than in the others; there is no perfected dwarf cherry as yet. The Malling IX is the runt of the litter. Its brothers and sisters, Malling numbers I, II, IV, VII, are somewhat larger, approaching semidwarfs. Pears are propagated exclusively on Anger Quince, which produces a most successful dwarf tree. It is also possible to buy peaches, plums, nectarines and apricots on dwarfing rootstocks.

The dwarf and semidwarf trees are really the answer for all of us who are going into this orchard business on a small scale for several reasons:

- Dwarf fruit trees usually begin to bear 1 or 2 years earlier than the standards.
- It takes less equipment to care for a dwarf orchard.
- Dwarfs can be pruned and trained more easily.
- Dwarfs grow one-third to half the height of standard trees.
- Because we can plant more trees in less space, we can cover several varieties and span the season more successfully with our crops.
- Because they are easier to maintain, dwarf trees will probably be better taken care of and the crop yield should be larger.

Plant in either late fall or early spring according to your climate. Full dwarf trees can be planted 10 to 12 feet apart each way; semidwarfs, 15 to 18 feet apart. The soil preparation, planting process and general tender loving care required are the same as for any sized fruit tree.

Incidentally, there is nothing dwarf about the fruit produced on these small trees. You can almost believe those glorious color photographs in the nursery catalogs, certainly enough to plant a few.

CHAPTER 3

····································
····································

ESPALIERS

To me, one of the most enjoyable aspects to planning and planting is the eye appeal. This is one of the few areas where you can enjoy your beauty and eat it too. Just one espaliered tree can be worth the whole project, especially if it is a pear tree placed against a sun-drenched wall, its green-leaved branches trained to display the greenish gold fruit that hangs so symmetrically from them. It is no wonder we see this motif used so often in American primitive painting. Its beauty is in its order and simplicity of design. If you have any of these characteristics in your nature, the espalier is for you.

Actually, an espalier is a fruit tree trained to grow flat against a wall, trellis or support of some kind. The rootstock for these trees is important as it determines the tree's later training. You

1

THREE FORMS OF ESPALIER

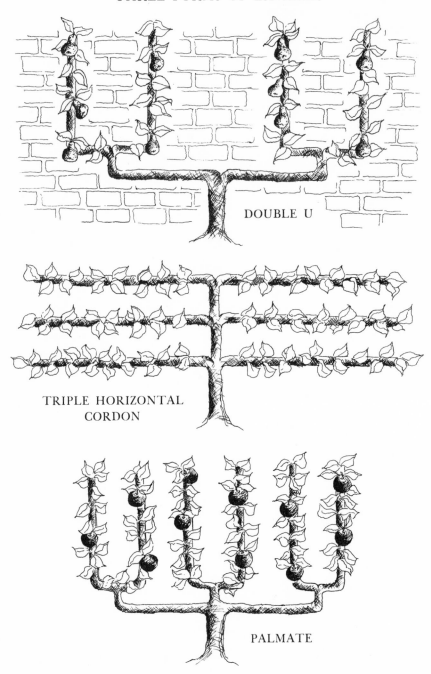

DOUBLE U

TRIPLE HORIZONTAL
CORDON

PALMATE

can buy standard dwarf trees, or there are a few nurseries that specialize in varieties just for espalier forms.

Espaliers are perfect covers for that large piece of white space that has been bothering you; and a simple horizontal cordon, which is a tree whose branches have been trained to grow along a straight fence, is the good housekeeper's answer to screening for that sometimes messy vegetable garden. A Belgian fence (a more complicated design) of apple and pear trees is a beautiful and professional accomplishment, and the garden house or gazebo made entirely of espaliered fruits could make you wish for a bevy of daughters and weddings. Just don't get as carried away with the art of espalier as a friend of mine did with the art of needlepoint. At last glance she had covered every piece of furniture and her husband in it. She can't stop.

By the way, espalier is a pruner's delight, as you can imagine. You even get a chance to prune in mid-summer!

::
::

CHAPTER 4

SEMITROPICAL AND TROPICAL FRUIT TREES

CITRUS FRUITS

A friend of mine has an orangerie. At least that is what he calls his glass-enclosed heated gazebo filled with semitropical plants. We occasionally have mid-winter picnics among the orange trees, gazing out at snow-covered meadows. It is a rather unreal setting, but the best we can do here in Connecticut. However, if you do live in a semitropical climate, you can plant a small citrus grove in the backyard under the open sky and picnic among the glossy-leaved trees almost all year 'round.

We have been so conditioned to frozen juices that we hardly think of the fruit itself as the source. The orange, probably the original "golden apple of the Hesperides," is one of nature's more handsome productions and is a good item with virtually no waste. The peel contains the flavorful oil sacs, the white portion of the peel contains pectin and other nutrients and even the seeds can be recycled into more orange trees.

All oranges come from two basic kinds—the sour and the sweet. The sour is the Seville, which is the ugliest orange of them all but the one that makes the best marmalade in the world—thick and dark, with a good bite to it. The Seville is rarely seen in the markets so it is well worth growing if you prefer that kind of marmalade on your toast or if you wish to forever endear yourself to your less fortunate northern friends. The tree also has beautiful, fragrant flowers. The sweet orange is with us all year long; if you live in California you need never be without oranges to squeeze for juice, to sauté in butter with cinnamon and sugar, to stuff and bake with raisins and honey, to pick off your own tree whenever the orange mood strikes you. Incidentally, a "tree-ripened" orange is the only kind there is. Citrus, unlike other fruit, does not ripen after picking.

Look into the Ponderosa lemon for an unusual, handsome and enormous (by ordinary market standards) lemon. It resembles the Italian lemon in size—some as big as small grapefruits. We might make use of some of the Italian tricks for seasoning food with this pungent juice—squeezing fresh lemon juice over freshly roasted meats, marinating vegetables in lemon juice, oil and lots of ground pepper, or putting a strip of peel in black coffee. We tend toward lemon pies and—proof of our English heritage—puddings. The lemon's sharp, clean, slightly acid flavor is a welcome contrast at the finish of a rich meal, and a lemon cheese pie with ripe strawberries can be the best of both worlds.

As with all fruits, there is a health advantage to growing your own citrus. Every school child is told about the high content of vitamin C in citrus fruit, and there is no doubt that the fresher the fruit, the more vitamin C it contains. And how much more pleasant it is to get vitamins in pie rather than pill form.

When I discovered that wonderful South American dish

named "Seviche," I envied my warm-weather friends their lime trees that produced such juicy fruit. The poor little limes in my market needed all the help I could give them in the way of boiling-water baths and massages to increase their juice volume. But it is worth the effort to produce this exciting flavorful dish of raw fish or seafood, highly spiced and "cooked" in the lime juice. It makes for elegant summer dining and is great for anyone who is on a diet.

With just a few trees the scent of orange blossoms can be heavy in the air and, if you don't feel as extravagant as Louis XIV, whose orangerie was the scene of masked balls and garden parties, you can just settle for iced tea and marmalade sandwiches under the blooming citrus trees.

SOIL

Citrus trees like well-drained or sandy loam soils. How often have you heard that? By now it must seem as if that is all you are allowed in the way of soil. Well, almost. If you haven't got it, make it (see page 24).

PLANTING

It is best to plant one- to two-year-old citrus trees because the larger trees will have too big a rootball and will not transplant as well. Planting should take place after all danger of frost is past, depending upon your own weather picture. Fear of frost is the one thing that keeps citrus growers awake at night—and rightly so. I know how I felt when a hurricane whipped across my hilltop orchard, and any such upset by Mother Nature is to be feared. However, when a severe frost has hit a particular geographic area, there is a preponderance of expert advice available on how to handle the damage. Usually, you cannot judge the extent of the damage for several months so there is nothing to be done immediately.

Do not be stingy with the space you allow each tree when planting; they like at least 15 feet around them. You will probably dig a bit more for these trees than for other fruit trees; the hole should be both deeper and wider than the rootball. Then refill to the depth of the ball for good drainage. If you have poor soil, dig large holes and backfill with good topsoil.

Place the tree in the hole without removing the ball covering, whatever it may be (it's usually burlap). If both burlap and tarpaper have been used, remove the tarpaper. Fill in the hole, firming it as you go. Leave a 2- to 4-inch-deep basin all around the trunk to facilitate irrigation. Use *no fertilizer* at planting time. A mulch is a good idea, and let the hose run a trickle of water into the basin immediately after planting to give the tree a good soaking. Remember that young trees need water more than anything else and you will have to be the judge of the amount they need. However, they probably should be watered every week or 10 days during the first year and about every two weeks for the next two or three years. It all depends on your climate, rainfall, sunshine, etc. Keep the 2- to 4-inch basins around the base of the trees and fill them with water periodically.

Since young citrus trees are delicate and tend to sunburn, the last step of the planting procedure is to wrap the trunks with cardboard. This also prevents any other injuries, such as lawn mower cuts, although by now you've probably decided that the lawn is an unnecessary nuisance and have done away with it.

MULCHING

Six to eight inches of mulch material will do the trick.

FERTILIZING

Nitrogen is the one major nutrient lacking in most soil. The sign that the tree needs nitrogen is a yellowing of the leaves. Use any commercial fertilizer that contains nitrogen and apply it by broadcasting evenly on the ground and beneath the tree. Water it in so it will be absorbed by the root system.

PRUNING

Supposedly, citrus trees do not need much pruning after planting and as they mature. Naturally, you will remove the sucker growth on the trunk or below the bud union when the trees are young. Then you will remove any inside shoot growth (shoots that grow between the junction of branches). If the trees grow too close to the house as they mature, you will have to cut back some limbs, and if the lower branches hang to the ground and get in the way of the lawn mower you will want to take them off. As lemon trees grow the most rapidly of all citrus, they will need moderate attention with the shears to slow their growth and increase their inside fruiting. All of this does not come under the heading of "pruning" as such, they say. It is just maintenance. Actually, even if you never prune a citrus tree it will take on a very nice, normal shape, so don't expend your energies on that part of its care.

INSECTS AND DISEASES

The most common disease striking the citrus tree is called "scaly bark" and it is a virus. Unfortunately, it is incurable at this time, but if you plant trees from registered "scaly-bark-free" parents you'll avoid it.

"Gummosis" is a fungus that causes the bark to die. You will notice it starting at or near ground level, and large amounts of gum will appear on the trunk. It usually occurs where the soil is wet for some length of time.

"Fruit drop" is a fairly common problem you will discover if you talk to your friends who are also cultivating citrus trees; not that this will make you feel any better if you are losing your crop. There are various reasons for this and you may have the problem one year and not the next, never knowing just what caused it. Again, good care with regard to watering, pruning and pest control will lessen the threat of fruit drop.

Naturally there are various pests—aphids, mites, thrips—that know a good thing when they see it. After all, they have to live also. They are not usually serious problems though. If you have an overdose of such insect life, however, consult your local agriculture station for help.

HARVESTING

As I mentioned earlier, citrus fruits do their ripening on the tree and can be left there for quite a while without deteriorating. The longer the fruit stays on the tree after maturity, the shorter the time it can be stored. When you want to pick the fruit be sure to handle with care. Gloves are recommended as you do not want a break in the rind and some fruits are quite thin-skinned. Clip; don't pull. Place fruits carefully in containers.

Storage temperature should be cool rather than cold—about sixty degrees. And here that old adage about the one rotten apple in the barrel seems particularly appropriate, even if we are mixing apples and oranges. One bad orange can speed decay of the whole lot, and the odor of rotting fruit can pervade the entire refrigerator. If you use the rind of the fruit, be sure to squeeze the juice and either drink it or store it in a glass container. If you have cut a lemon or orange in half, put the cut half into a container with ½ inch of water in the bottom, cut side up; cover and refrigerate.

VARIETIES

The types of citrus you plant will depend on your location in the Sunbelt. Professional growers can advise you as to which ones will do best.

Navel oranges with their zip-off skins are wonderful for eating, as are the Murcotts. Valencias give a rich orange-hued juice and are one of the most widely grown varieties. Temples are a combination of orange and tangerine with the best qualities of both. There are also the famous blood oranges, which unfortunately have almost disappeared. According to one authority, "they frighten American women." These delicious and spectacular oranges grow well in Florida.

The Meyer lemon tree is the recommended variety for home orchards because of its cold hardiness and its small size.

Grapefruit generally falls into two classifications—Marsh for California and Duncan for Florida—with acknowledgments paid to the Texas Ruby.

Florida has the corner on the commercial lime market, probably because of all citrus the lime has the least tolerance to cold. But there are a few varieties that will grow in certain parts of California.

There are many other varieties of citrus and their kissin' cousins, such as Kumquats, Calamondins, Tangerines and the Mandarins, all worth experimenting with if you live in what the chamber of commerce likes to call a "sunshine state."

RECIPES

Aunt Bet's Blender Lemon Soup

I do not usually advocate canned soups, but this is particularly well flavored and delightful for a summer luncheon with a seafood and avocado salad, iced tea and hot biscuits.

4 SERVINGS

1 can (10 ounces) cream of chicken soup
1 can (10 ounces) chicken broth
1 cup light cream
Juice of 2 lemons
3 tablespoons chopped mint
Chopped parsley to garnish
Salt to taste
Freshly ground black pepper to taste

Pour cream of chicken soup, broth, light cream and lemon juice into blender container. Puree until smooth. Add mint and turn blender on and then immediately off. Chill for 4 to 5 hours and serve with parsley garnish. Add salt and pepper to taste.

Poached Oranges

2 navel oranges
1 cup sugar
½ cup water

Peel oranges, removing all white pith underneath skin. Cut each orange into 4 slices. Bring sugar and water to a boil in a small saucepan, dissolving sugar. Simmer uncovered and add orange slices, 4 at a time. Poach for 10 minutes, until oranges are soft but have not lost their shape. Remove to bowl. Repeat for remaining slices.

Poached Oranges with Orange Cream

4 SERVINGS

3 egg yolks
⅓ cup sugar
¼ cup orange juice
¼ cup orange liqueur
½ cup cream, whipped
2 poached navel oranges, sliced
Grated rind of 1 orange

Combine yolks, sugar and orange juice in heavy saucepan. Cook over medium heat, stirring until mixture thickens. Remove from heat and very slowly whisk in liqueur. Let cool. Fold in whipped cream and chill. Just before serving, arrange poached orange slices in serving dish and pour cream over them. Garnish with grated rind.

Glazed Poached Orange Slices

4 SERVINGS

2 poached navel oranges, sliced
1 teaspoon cinnamon
¼ cup sugar
Strawberries to garnish

Arrange orange slices in flat baking dish. Combine cinnamon and sugar and sprinkle cinnamon-sugar mixture evenly over orange slices. Glaze under hot broiler, 3 inches from flame, until bubbly. Garnish with strawberries and serve at once.

Poached Orange Bread Pudding

This is a grown-up bread pudding—far from the one served by Nanny in the nursery.

10 SERVINGS

2 poached navel oranges, sliced
2 tablespoons amber or dark rum
Butter, softened
10 small, thin slices French bread
3 cups milk
¾ cup light cream
1 cup sugar
4 eggs
3 egg yolks
¼ cup confectioners' sugar

Preheat oven to 375°. While orange slices are still warm, put them in a bowl with the rum. Butter one side of bread slices. Combine milk and cream in saucepan and heat until scalded. Remove from heat and stir in sugar. Beat in eggs and yolks. Butter a 3-quart shallow baking dish. Drain oranges, reserve rum and add it to custard mixture. Arrange orange slices on bottom of baking dish. Place bread slices, buttered side down, over oranges. Pour custard over all. Place dish in pan of hot water and bake for 40 to 50 minutes until set. Let stand at room temperature. Before serving, sprinkle confectioners' sugar over top and glaze briefly under broiler, 3 inches under flame.

Orange Walnut Chicken

4 SERVINGS

2 tablespoons butter
1 tablespoon oil
2 shallots, minced
3 whole chicken breasts, split
Flour for dredging
Salt to taste
Freshly ground pepper to taste
½ teaspoon ground ginger
3 tablespoons orange liqueur
1 cup orange juice
½ cup dry white wine
Grated rind of 1 orange
1 cup toasted walnut pieces

In a large skillet, heat butter and oil. Add shallots and sauté for 2 to 3 minutes. Dry chicken breasts and dredge with flour, salt, pepper and ginger. Sauté breasts in skillet until golden on all sides. Remove to ovenproof dish and flame with liqueur. Pour orange juice into skillet and bring to a boil, stirring. Pour over chicken. Add wine. Cover and simmer over low heat for 30 minutes. Ten minutes before serving, sprinkle with orange rind and toasted walnuts.

Hot Russian Tea

3½ CUPS

3 teaspoons Darjeeling tea
½ teaspoon whole cloves
1 stick cinnamon, 2 inches long
1 strip orange peel, 3 inches long
½ cup honey
3 cups boiling water
Lemon wedges
Whole cloves

Put tea, spices, orange peel and honey into pitcher. Pour boiling water over and steep for 5 minutes. Strain. Serve with lemon wedges studded with additional whole cloves.

Cold Lemon Chicken

4 SERVINGS

2 egg yolks
1 cup heavy cream
1 tablespoon butter
¼ cup sherry
2 large chicken breasts, split, boned, skinned and cooked
Grated rind of 1 large or 2 small lemons
Watercress, lemon slices and small black olives to garnish

In top of double boiler, beat yolks and cream together. Place over simmering water and add butter and sherry. Cook, stirring, until slightly thickened. Place cooked chicken breasts on serving platter and pour sauce over them. Sprinkle with lemon rind. Cover and refrigerate. Before serving, garnish platter with cress, lemon slices and olives. Serve chilled.

Italian Zucchini

4 TO 6 SERVINGS

3 to 4 zucchini squash, unpeeled and cut into 1/4-inch
rounds (about 1 1/2 pounds zucchini)
Olive oil
Freshly ground pepper to taste
Juice of 1 lemon

Cook zucchini until barely tender in boiling salted water to
barely cover. Drain and dry on paper towels. Place zucchini
rounds in flat baking dish and sprinkle with oil, lightly coating
each piece. Sprinkle generously with black pepper. Cover and
let stand 3 to 4 hours. Just before serving, squeeze fresh lemon
juice over all.

Lemon Black Walnut Soufflé

4 SERVINGS

5 egg yolks
3/4 cup sugar
Grated rind of 1/2 lemon
1/4 cup lemon juice
1/2 cup finely chopped black walnuts
6 egg whites
1/8 teaspoon salt

Preheat oven to 350°. In mixing bowl, beat yolks until light,
gradually adding sugar. Beat until thick and creamy. Beat in
lemon rind and juice. Fold in nuts. Beat whites with salt until
stiff. Fold into yolk mixture. Pour mixture into buttered 1 1/2-
quart soufflé dish. Set dish in pan of hot water. Bake for 40 to 45
minutes until firm. Serve at once.

Lemon Slice Pie

2 lemons, sliced paper thin
2 cups sugar
Pastry for two 8-inch piecrusts
4 eggs
1 teaspoon sugar

Place lemon slices in bowl, removing seeds. Stir sugar into lemon slices and let stand overnight.

Preheat oven to 425°. Roll out half of pastry and fit into pie pan. Prick bottom and sides with fork. Bake for 8 to 10 minutes. Cool.

Beat eggs and stir into lemon mixture. Pour into pie shell. Roll out remaining pastry and fit over top of pie. Sprinkle with 1 teaspoon sugar. Bake for 10 minutes at 450°. Reduce heat to 350° and bake for 30 to 40 minutes longer, until a knife thrust into the center comes out clean. Cool before serving.

Lemon Cheese Pie

1 graham cracker crust for 8-inch piecrust
3 packages (3 ounces each) cream cheese, softened
2 tablespoons butter
½ cup sugar
1 egg
2 tablespoons flour
⅔ cup milk
¼ cup lemon juice
2 tablespoons grated lemon rind
Ripe strawberries, hulled, to garnish

Preheat oven to 350°. Press piecrust in pie pan. In bowl, beat together the cream cheese and butter until smooth. Beat in sugar and egg. Add flour and milk, blending well. Stir in lemon juice and rind.

Pour into pie shell and bake for 30 minutes until firm. Cool and garnish with strawberries.

Lemon Curd

ABOUT 1 CUP

2 tablespoons butter
⅔ cup sugar
2 eggs
¼ cup lemon juice
Grated rind of 1 lemon

Melt butter in top of double boiler over simmering water. Stir in sugar and eggs, beating well. Add lemon juice and rind and cook, stirring, until thick and smooth. Cool.

This will keep several days in the refrigerator and is very useful as filling for cakes, muffins, cream puffs or tarts.

Cupcakes with Lemon Curd Filling

2 DOZEN CUPCAKES

1 cup lemon curd (see above)
½ cup butter
1¾ cups sugar
5 egg yolks
2¾ cups flour
½ teaspoon salt
2½ teaspoons baking powder
⅔ cup milk
1 teaspoon vanilla or ½ teaspoon almond extract
3 egg whites
Confectioners' sugar

Preheat oven to 350°. Cream butter, adding sugar gradually, until light and smooth. Add yolks and beat well. Mix flour, salt and baking powder and add alternately with milk to butter-yolk mixture. Stir in vanilla or almond extract. In another bowl, beat egg whites until stiff but not dry and fold in. Fill well-greased muffin tins ¾ full. Bake on center shelf of oven until lightly browned, about 15 to 18 minutes. Remove cakes at once to racks. With a sharp knife, remove tops of cakes and set aside. Scoop out a small amount of crumb and fill with lemon curd. Replace tops and dust with confectioners' sugar.

Seviche

SERVES 4 FOR LUNCH, 6 AS A FIRST COURSE

1 pound scallops
⅔ cup lime juice
6 tablespoons olive oil
3 tablespoons finely chopped onion
6 tablespoons chopped parsley
1 garlic clove, minced
2 tablespoons finely chopped, peeled canned green chiles
1 teaspoon salt
Freshly ground pepper to taste
Dash of Tabasco
1 tablespoon capers, drained

If scallops are large, cut them into pieces the size of bay scallops. Put them in a bowl with lime juice and refrigerate for 4 hours. Drain. Mix together all of the remaining 9 ingredients except 3 tablespoons of parsley and toss gently with scallops. Refrigerate until ready to serve. Garnish with remaining parsley.

This is a refreshing, nonfattening first course or luncheon dish.

Fresh Grapefruit and Scallop Shells

6 SERVINGS

1 pound scallops
1 cup dry white wine
Salt to taste
2 large grapefruits, peeled, sectioned and seeded
¼ cup melted butter or margarine
Paprika to taste
1 tablespoon chopped parsley

Preheat oven to 350°. If scallops are large, cut them into ¼-inch pieces. Put scallops into saucepan with ⅔ cup wine and salt. Cover and simmer 3 to 5 minutes until scallops are opaque. Drain well. Cut grapefruit sections in half and combine with scallops. Fill individual scallop shells with this mixture. Combine remaining wine with butter. Spoon over each filled shell. Sprinkle with paprika and parsley. Bake for 5 to 6 minutes. Serve at once.

PERSIMMONS

Romantically named the "fruit of Jove," the persimmon seems to be all things to all who are lucky enough to be able to cultivate it. It is extremely ornamental in an Oriental manner (its origins are Oriental) ; it grows to the pleasant height of about 30 feet with wide, spreading branches that are nice to sit under. In the spring the new leaves are a soft, lightish green; with growth they become large, dark and a bit leathery (good for flower arrangements) ; in the fall they turn the most glorious shades of red, yellow and orange. After this, you might think the tree had given its all, but no! Stunning bright orange fruits appear and for a short time the whole tree looks as if it is bedecked with tiny Japanese lanterns all aglow. And, of course, its final contribution to your well-being is delicious fruit to eat raw in a salad or use in puddings, pies, jams and cakes. I don't believe that there is another fruit quite so handsome and decorative to work with, due to its marvelous striking color. A few slices of persimmon with avocado and citrus on a bed of greens would take a prize in any art class.

Furthermore, this tree is easy to grow and the fruit has good nutritive value, containing a high percentage of glucose and protein. However, as there is no such thing as a Garden of Eden, there must be one drawback. Except for the Fuyu, all varieties of persimmon are astringent and sour until fully ripe. That old expression about setting your teeth on edge would apply here. But I have eaten a half-ripe Fuyu right from the tree without a pucker. There is a way to remove the astringency if you are in a hurry and can't wait for ripening, which might take several days. Place the firm fruit in the freezer for about 24 hours. When it thaws, it will be soft, nonastringent and can, or should, be used immediately.

I would encourage anyone to try a persimmon tree. We do

not see enough of them in this country and besides, it's always fun to be the first one on the block with something new and different. They are self-fruitful so you do not have to plan on a pair of these quite large trees.

SOIL

Persimmons are not fussy about their soil and will grow quite well on dry soil, sandy soil or limestone. However, if you're going to encourage them with the best conditions, a good clay loam, fresh and deep, with good drainage is preferred. The Oriental persimmon, which is probably the one you will choose as opposed to the American persimmon, can be grown in subtropical and temperate areas, generally areas where citrus, figs, olives, almonds and peaches also grow.

PLANTING

The persimmon tree has an extensive root system and care must be taken when transplanting. Be sure to set the tree in the ground at the same depth it was in the nursery and keep the roots well protected before it is in the ground. Be sure to water the newly planted tree well, immediately after filling in the hole. If your soil is deep, the trees should be planted between 20 and 25 feet apart, depending upon the variety you select.

MULCHING

Since it's always a good idea to mulch, treat this tree as you would any other tree in your orchard.

FERTILIZING

Persimmons like nitrogen, but not too much. Overfeeding will cause excess growth and excess fruit drop. The fertilizing should be done consistently in the late winter or early spring. A rule of thumb for the mature tree is 1 to 1½ pounds of nitrogen per year, depending upon the makeup of the soil.

PRUNING

Here again, you get a break on pruning—or perhaps not, if you really love to use those shears. Just take care of the dead or damaged branches, and, if there seems to be too much interior growth, thin it out to let in the air.

INSECTS AND DISEASES

While it is never possible to say there will be no insects and diseases, the persimmon may very well be the ideal tree in that there is nothing here to seriously consider or worry about.

HARVESTING

Firm fruits should be left on the tree until they develop a good color. Good color—gorgeous orange—is the criterion and it is easy to spot. If the fruit is picked while immature it may not ripen evenly and will not lose all of its astringency. Clip the fruit from the branch, leaving a short stem attached. Handle carefully to avoid bruises.

Persimmons can be kept for quite a while in a cool place. They can also be frozen. The best way to do this is to peel and puree them, pack the pulp in airtight containers and then freeze. Supposedly, they can also be frozen whole in plastic bags, but I have never tried this method. I did try freezing tomatoes whole and was not pleased with the soggy results. But the idea of freezing the pulp is a good one. If you're overwhelmed with a lot of dead ripe persimmons and have neither the time nor the inclination to use them immediately, this is one way of storing them for that rainy day when you do have some time.

VARIETIES

Choose from among the Oriental persimmons since they produce a more satisfactory fruit for the home grower.

Fuyu: A large persimmon with orange-red color. It is non-astringent

Hachiya: This is a large, acorn-shaped persimmon, deep orange-red in color

Tenashi: A persimmon more widely grown in the southern states

RECIPES

Persimmon Pie

1½ tablespoons flour
⅓ cup sugar
Grated rind of 1 lemon
Grated rind of ½ orange
½ teaspoon cinnamon
¼ teaspoon ground cloves
½ teaspoon nutmeg
4 cups peeled and sliced persimmons (fruit should be firm, not jelly-like)
1 tablespoon butter
1 tablespoon light cream
Pastry for two 9-inch piecrusts

Preheat oven to 450°. Roll out pastry and fit half into pie pan. In bowl, mix together the flour, sugar, fruit rinds and spices. Fold in persimmons. Spoon filling into pan. Dot with butter. Cover with pastry top crust. Brush crust with cream. Put pie on bottom shelf of oven and bake for 10 minutes. Turn heat down to 350° and place pie on center shelf. Bake for 40 to 45 minutes longer until browned and bubbling.

Persimmon Parfait

6 SERVINGS

3 egg yolks
4 tablespoons confectioners' sugar
⅓ cup orange liqueur
1 cup heavy whipping cream
1½ cups persimmon pulp
1 tablespoon grated lemon rind
3 tablespoons lemon juice
Sugar to taste
Salted cashews, chopped, to garnish

Beat egg yolks and confectioners' sugar until thick and lemon colored. Beat in liqueur in small amounts. In another bowl, whip cream until stiff and combine with yolk mixture. Freeze for several hours until stiff. Combine persimmon pulp with lemon rind, juice and sugar. Cover and chill for several hours. To serve, layer the two mixtures in tall glasses and sprinkle chopped salted cashew nuts over top.

FIGS

Anyone who has taken a course in ancient history, read Cicero or studied the Bible in even a cursory fashion has noted the frequent mention of figs and fig trees. It is said that Romulus and Remus were found under a fig tree, and the tree itself symbolizes prosperity and well-being. This is probably as good a reason as any for planting one. There are other perhaps more valid reasons, however, such as the shade it gives, its ornamental appearance and its beautiful fruits, which can be eaten fresh with thinly sliced prosciutto ham, stuffed with other foods from the Middle East (nuts and honey) and then baked or used as a garnish for small birds or ducks.

We do not do much with fig trees in this country. The expression "I don't give a fig" aptly describes our attitude. Too bad, because it is an interesting tree to work with, and, not being a truly tropical tree, it can survive low temperatures. Actually, it is possible to plant fig trees successfully in containers in the Northeast if you take them inside during the winter.

Essentially, one must like figs to consider putting in this tree. If you've been under the impression that you don't, try some recipes first, using both the fresh and the dried fruits, and find out how you really feel about this ancient, biblical fruit. You may be very surprised. It is hard to resist the combination of fresh figs and ham, arranged decoratively on a chilled platter and served on the terrace under the green shade of the fig tree on a bright autumn day. A chilled glass of white wine and some good bread and cheese complete the perfect lunch.

SOIL

For once, I don't have to recommend perfect soil. This tree is not fussy as long as it gets full sun and good drainage.

PLANTING

There are a few rules to follow when planting fig trees. One rule is never to plant over the septic tank drain fields, as the roots of these trees can get into the system, and then you have real trouble. Another good rule is to pick a sunny spot away from competing trees and shrubs. Fig trees tend to do well when planted about 4 feet from a southern wall because the reflected heat is just what they like to grow on—and on and on. If you have such a location, you might consider espaliering the tree; with a small brick or gravel terrace, a few benches and a table, you will have created the perfect setting for that autumn luncheon.

If you plant the tree bare-rooted (with uncovered roots), prune ⅓ off the top (unless this has been done in the nursery). A container-grown tree goes in the ground as is—no pruning.

Set the tree in the hole 3 to 4 inches deeper than it was in the nursery. After filling in with soil, be sure to water heavily to settle the soil around the roots. Like most fruit trees, figs benefit from adequate watering. As time goes by, observation will tell you how things are going in that department. If shoot growth continues and the leaves look healthy and are a proper size, then your tree is getting enough moisture.

Remember that the fig is a very shallow rooted tree and any deep cultivation could damage the root system. A point to consider when planting is that the roots tend to spread out farther than the branches. Allow 20 feet or more between trees. If space is a consideration but you are carried away by the Apician romance of figs, look into the new dwarf fig trees. They can be a lot of fun to work with.

MULCHING

Start mulching right away, putting on hay, sawdust or pine needles, 4 to 6 inches from the tree trunk out beyond the tips of the branches.

FERTILIZING

If your soil is moderately fertile, these trees do not need extra fertilizers.

PRUNING

Except in California, the fig tree is better off as a fig bush, so prune accordingly. In case of a freeze a bush, which has more than one main leader, has a better chance of survival than a lonely-leadered tree.

By cutting off ⅓ of the top at planting time, you are forcing shoots to grow from the base of the plant. Let the shoots grow through the first season. The following winter, pick out three or more vigorous shoots, widely spaced, to be the leaders. Remove all other shoots and prune the chosen leaders to within one foot of the ground. When you choose your leaders, remember that they will grow 3 to 4 inches in diameter. If for some reason one of these primary leaders does get damaged, remove it and pick a new one from the suckers that will appear each year.

The second year, while the tree is dormant, remove about ⅓ to ½ of its annual growth. This is called "heading back" the bush and will turn the erstwhile tree into a bush, giving it a shape. Also, prune all dead wood and sucker growth. Make all pruning cuts back to a bud or branch so as not to leave bare stubs.

INSECTS AND DISEASES

The main pest problem for these trees is the "nematode," a scientific name for a tiny soil worm that goes at the roots. If successful, it can kill the young tree or at least stunt its growth and can produce fruit drop in the mature tree. Here again, ask for expert advice if you have this problem because using the wrong chemicals could do more damage than the nematodes.

HARVESTING

Figs are not good to eat until they are fully ripe, and at that point they tend to deteriorate quickly, so make sure you're around when the crop comes to maturity. Actually, because they have a very high sugar content, they will dry very well. You don't have to go on a diet of the ripe fruit just to use it up. Fruit drop can be a problem so don't place your dining table directly under the tree. That might result in too much of a good thing.

VARIETIES

Brown Turkey: The fig with the longest ripening season
Celeste: Relatively small figs
Kadota: An excellent fig for canning

RECIPES

Baked Stuffed Figs

4 TO 6 SERVINGS

    12 slightly underripe figs
    ½ cup cream cheese, softened
    4 teaspoons chopped crystalized ginger
    4 tablespoons chopped almonds
    ¼ cup Port wine
    2 tablespoons honey

Preheat oven to 350°. Cut off top ⅓ of figs and hollow out slightly; reserve tops. Cream together the cream cheese, ginger, and almonds. Fill each fig with some of the cheese mixture and put tops back on. Stand figs in a lightly greased, shallow baking dish. In a small saucepan, heat together the wine and honey and pour over figs. Bake until figs are soft, basting frequently, for about 20 minutes. Chill overnight. Serve cold.

Game Hens with Figs

4 SERVINGS

12 figs, halved
Port wine
2 tablespoons butter
1 tablespoon oil
2 Cornish game hens, split
1 ounce brandy
Salt to taste
Freshly ground pepper to taste
3 tablespoons orange juice concentrate

Preheat oven to 350°. Soak figs in wine overnight. Heat butter and oil in large skillet and sauté game hens on both sides until golden. Heat brandy, pour over hens, and flame. Sprinkle hens with salt and pepper and remove to baking dish. Drain wine from figs into skillet. Add orange juice concentrate. Bring to a boil, stirring, and pour over hens. Cover and bake for 30 minutes. Add figs and bake for 10 minutes longer. Serve game hens garnished with the fig halves.

Fig Conserve

6 TO 8 JARS (8 OUNCES EACH)

½ lemon, very thinly sliced
4 cups figs, very thinly sliced
1½ cups sugar
1 cup chopped walnuts
½ cup chopped dates
½ cup brandy or rum

Remove seeds from lemon slices. Put figs and lemons into large saucepan with sugar. Bring to a boil, reduce heat and simmer until thick, about 45 to 60 minutes. Stir constantly. Remove from heat and stir in nuts, dates, and brandy or rum. Pour into sterilized jars and seal, following the Instructions for Preserving on page 185.

AVOCADOS

Presumably, a gardener should be so concerned with the miracles of growth and should be so appreciative of nature's timely manners that he has no time for envy or unfruitful wishing. So it is only on rare occasions that I permit myself the luxury of "if only" thoughts. But when I do, it is dreams of ripe avocados that dance in my head. If only I didn't have to buy my avocados rockhard for 79 cents apiece. If only I could pick them ripe from my own tree whenever I wanted a salad of avocado and seafood vinaigrette; a fiery guacamole to scoop up with corn chips; a creamy, lemony cold soup or a beauty treatment in the form of a shampoo or facial.

This hand-me-down from the Spaniards could easily be the answer to the riddle: What looks like a pear, but tastes like a nut; grows on a tree, but is used as a vegetable; is a natural "convenience food" with a high energy content? The avocado is both soul-satisfying and conscience-soothing in that it allows us to indulge ourselves in a very sensual food while still getting extra health benefits; it's a "nutritionally wise investment of calories" as one devotee remarked.

The avocado is also a big handsome tree that flourishes in both Florida and California, given the right conditions and enough room to grow. So, if you're that lucky, plant one.

SOIL

Avocados can grow in a wide range of soils, but that good old familiar, well-drained, medium-textured soil is best.

PLANTING

The avocado is budded on seedlings and these budded trees are grown one year and transplanted the following spring. You will probably buy them balled from the nursery as one-year trees. They should be planted at least 30 feet apart as you're talking about a possible height of 40 feet. As for time of planting, in California good months are December to February; in Florida fall planting during late September and October is preferable. If you plant any later than that you must watch the watering closely. At planting time, do not prune the avocado except for suckers below the graft union. Do wrap or whitewash the trunks for sunburn prevention.

MULCHING

Mulch as you would any tree in your orchard.

FERTILIZING

The avocado has the same requirements for nourishment as the citrus, which makes the cultivation convenient. And it also makes sense (nature usually does), as their climatic conditions are very similar. Early growth is encouraged by doses of organic nitrogen, which can be broadcast uniformly beneath the trees.

PRUNING

If you pruned away any suckers when you planted your trees—
and by now that has become an automatic reaction—then these
trees will not need any extra attention along this line except for
taking out damaged and weak limbs. Since the tree grows to
such great heights, this is just as well—one less hazard to contend
with. In any case, I'm told that you should never prune in hot
weather.

INSECTS AND DISEASES

Good, healthy avocado trees seldom suffer from either of these
problems. The most serious condition you might face is "avocado root rot," and this is usually a result of poorly drained
soil. As there is no cure for this, it behooves you not to plant
under such conditions; and if you have read through the book
to this point, I am sure you won't.

HARVESTING

Unfortunately, you cannot just run out to the tree five minutes
before lunch and grab a ripe avocado for the salad. These fruits
do not soften on the tree and you cannot tell the time of maturity by size alone. The purple or dark varieties are usually
mature when the fruit starts to turn from green to dark. With
green-skin varieties the bright green color lessens and a yellowish hue appears. I remember with amusement (because it was
not my problem) a friend telling me about the year when every
avocado on the tree seemed to ripen at once. They ate it, drank
it, baked it, broiled it, mashed it, wore it and froze it.

When taking the fruit from the tree, cut and don't pull the
avocado from its stem. Avocados mature according to climate,
location and variety, so you should find all this out when you
pick out your trees at the nursery.

VARIETIES

Choosing which variety of avocado you would like for your very
own can be confusing as there are several hundred types avail-

able. A good guideline would be to find out which kinds are grown commercially near you. Obviously, these are well tested and should give you the same good results. The experts advise, if you are not near commercial groves, to pick varieties that will produce fruit under possible adverse chilling conditions. This will minimize your losses and your worries.

Incidentally, in California there are both summer and winter avocados—the best of both worlds. Fuerte, with its bright green skin, is the best known of the winter varieties. Hass is a dark pebbly-skinned fruit that is smaller in size and bears in the summer. A note for weight watchers: Summer avocados have roughly twice the calories of winter avocados.

RECIPES

Cold Avocado Soup

6 TO 8 SERVINGS

 3 large avocados
 3 cups chicken bouillon
 1 cup peeled, seeded and diced cucumbers
 ¼ cup chopped scallions
 1 clove garlic, peeled
 3 tablespoons lemon juice
 1½ teaspoons salt
 Dash Tabasco
 Freshly ground pepper to taste
 3 tomatoes, peeled and chopped

Put all ingredients except tomatoes in blender and puree until smooth. Chill. Serve chilled and garnish with chopped tomato.

Guacamole

ABOUT 2 CUPS

3 ripe avocados, mashed with fork or pureed
1 tablespoon grated onion
2 tablespoons lemon or lime juice
3 canned green chiles, seeded and finely chopped
Salt to taste
1 clove garlic, minced
Dash of Tabasco

Mix avocado with all other ingredients. Cover and chill.

- Serve as salad garnished with sliced tomatoes or as filling for hollowed-out tomato cases.
- Spread on toasted sourdough bread and cover with cooked bacon slices.
- Use as a sauce on fish, chicken or tongue.
- Put a tablespoonful on a bowl of gazpacho.
- Spoon onto hot grilled lamb chops.
- Combine with meat loaf in a sandwich.

Avocado Half-Shells

6 SERVINGS

1 can (3 ounces) small shrimp
1 can (12 ounces) consommé madrilene
1 tablespoon lemon juice
Salt to taste
Freshly ground pepper to taste
1 tablespoon chopped chives
3 avocados, unpeeled
1 cup sour cream
Chopped parsley to garnish

Drain and rinse shrimp. Combine with madrilene, lemon juice, salt, pepper and chives. Chill overnight until set. Halve and pit avocados and spoon jelled mixture into shells. Garnish with sour cream and parsley.

Carol's Avocado Dessert

2 TO 3 SERVINGS

> 2 dead-ripe avocados
> Sugar
> 1 pitcherful of lime juice

Peel and mash avocados and place in small dessert dishes just before serving. Pass a bowl of sugar and a pitcher of lime juice. Add sugar and lime according to taste and stir into avocado pulp.

The Avocado Masque Beauty Treatment

> ½ avocado, mashed
> 1 tablespoon honey
> ¼ cup milk

Mix avocado, honey and milk in a blender.

Wash your face and neck thoroughly and apply the mixture to your skin. Lie down and relax for 20 minutes. Remove with tepid water and a cloth.

Avocado Shampoo

> ½ cup regular shampoo
> ½ cup water
> ½ avocado pulp

Pour shampoo and water into the blender. Add the avocado pulp and blend on "high" for 10 seconds. Wash your hair with this mixture. Rinse with warm water until hair no longer feels sticky.

PART TWO

Patches and Vines

There was a time in these United States when berries grew and flourished in great abundance. Indeed, when a family went picnicking they could be assured of fresh fruit for dessert by simply doing a bit of berry picking. Unfortunately, this is not so any longer and, as we see the pathetically small amount of fresh berries that are available in our markets (at an ever-increasing price), it does not take much imagination to figure out how to satisfy our taste for these small fruits. Berries are not hard to grow; that is, the brambles, which would still be rambling wildly over the countryside if the countryside had been left in its natural state, are not hard to grow. As our population grows so do our problems, but it is nice to know that on any size lot we can plant and cultivate some of the berries that are virtually unknown to a new generation.

For instance, how often do you see gooseberries, boysenberries or dewberries for sale? Perhaps you've never even tasted any of these small fruits and a gooseberry tart is just a mysterious mention in an English novel. As for boysenberry or dewberry jelly or wine, you'll have to put in a bush or two and make use of your own perfectly ripened berries if you want to have the pleasure of tasting these.

It is virtually impossible for any commercial grower to deliver his produce to the customer at the peak of ripeness. No fruit is more perishable than the small berry and, with the exception of the blueberry, it is not economically feasible for large growers to attempt the marketing of these berries. It is through our own sense of taste and smell that we know when a berry is at the right stage for picking. As a matter of fact, during the raspberry season I eat my breakfast right off the bushes. We pick just before we are about to use the berries and this is as it should be for perfect flavor and texture.

Here we should consider the nutrition angle, which touches us all these days and is possibly one of the main reasons why we are so interested in growing the foods that will nourish our bodies. There is virtually no reason to use poisonous sprays on berry bushes, so the fruit need not be touched by anything other than your own loving hands.

Economy is certainly not the least of our concerns, and berry bushes come under the "good buy" category. Once bought and planted, they will go on and on. The initial investment is not enormous, considering the great variety offered by the growers with new types constantly appearing on the markets. Another type of economical consideration might also enter into this planning—economy of space. We all have visions of berry patches taking over the grounds; we assume that we need acres of land to just let them ramble. Actually, I sometimes think that too much open space just leads to wastefulness and a tendency to "let go," whereas if we must conserve we will make better use of what we've got. This is a long-winded way of saying that berries can be planted very neatly and tidily on a small piece of land and will thrive. You might just adopt the philosophy of a friend of mine who regards lawn as an unnecessary evil and is gradually covering it with gardens of all sorts—less to mow and more to enjoy and eat.

"Vineyard" can be an awesome word when applied to the average homestead. It would be better to think of having a few grapevines trained on wires, an arbor or a trellis. Six to twelve plants would be enough. Assuming that you live in a climate conducive to growing grapes—that is, almost anywhere in the United States except the extremely cold northern states—you can grow any of the three varieties, or cultivars, available.

Considering that rhubarb is one of nature's oldest plants, dating back to 2700 B.C., it took a long time for it to become part of our daily diet. Purportedly the first rhubarb entered America by way of Maine in the seventeenth century, but it still wasn't used extensively due to the scarcity of sugar; and if there is one thing this plant calls for it is sweetening. Rhubarb may readily be called New England's plant as it takes to the climate of cold winters naturally and seems to be the perfect ingredient for hearty, warming desserts, such as deep-dish pies, crumbles and baked puddings.

Practicality is fine and necessary, but the impracticalities of our own natures must be considered also. It is just plain exciting to grow varieties of fruits that we have heard about but have never seen or tasted. There is always something new under the sun even if it is simply a new thornless version of an old prickly fruit. When you go through the catalogs and see all of the endless experimentation that the plant growers are doing, you are bound to share the feelings of excitement derived from producing a new species of fruit or berry. This alone is reason enough for growing these delightful fruits.

CHAPTER 5

BERRY PATCHES

STRAWBERRIES

There are certain fruits that are truly "sweet to the eye and mind" and the strawberry is one of these. If it were not so perishable it would be the most decorative item we could keep around during its season. However, it should be eaten at its peak of ripeness. Because of its natural beauty, we buy replicas of the strawberry on everything from strawberry motif pots to pillows for our admiration during the rest of the year. We eat the fruit as soon as possible after picking for purely selfish reasons—the supreme enjoyment of biting into a sun-warmed, sweet juicy berry. But we also manage to get an extra benefit in the form of large amounts of vitamin C, which remain in the berry for just a short time after harvest (so much for shipping this perishable fruit across the country in the middle of winter) .

Actually, the strawberry is a member of the rose family. More importantly, there are fewer and fewer local farmers raising berries because of the labor problems—they must be hand-picked. It would behoove you to put a strawberry bed in your own backyard just for that reason alone. Quite honestly, these are not the easiest berries you could raise from the point of view of time required. The rewards are worth the effort, though, when you taste the first shortcake of the season that has been made with old-fashioned unsweetened biscuits drenched in ripe strawberries and served in a soup bowl with softly whipped cream poured over the whole thing. My stockbroker-gardening friend Charlie says that he has to keep thinking of that short-cake when it comes to his strawberry bed; he knows that every third year it will have to be completely replanted if he's going to do it right, and that can take the best part of a day.

As your strawberry bed continues to present you with quarts of berries every day (especially the second year), you can in-dulge in homemade ice cream made with just berries, sugar and heavy cream, or the biggest and most beautiful berries sprinkled with sugar and wine. You might experiment with one of the many versions of Strawberries Romanoff or, as a sop to your conscience, enjoy a light and low-calorie strawberry ice. And, of course, you can always park the children out on the road under an umbrella with baskets of ripe strawberries to sell, pro-vided they do the picking themselves. Exercise some control over this, however; Charlie has never forgotten the year he didn't eat one of his own strawberries because the children sold them all.

Also, when you take on strawberries you are entering into a family situation because each mother plant produces runners that grow into plants the following season. As you can see, strawberries can be a profitable crop to cultivate.

Strawberries are decorative on the ground as well as on the plate, so think about where you might put them for looks as well as convenience.

We all have several favorite fruits; during the harvest seasons we tend to jump from one to the other like faithless lovers rushing from one romance to the next, convinced that each is the only one in the world. Unlike these peripatetic Romeos, we should find room in our lives for enough of each to satisfy our demands and spend the summer months feasting quite happily on fruits and berries of all kinds.

SOIL

Strawberries like and deserve a bed of their own to lie in. It should be a bed prepared especially for them with no traces of leftover vegetables, such as tomatoes, potatoes, eggplant, corn or peppers. So if you were planning to cut down on your vegetable production, as all gardeners do at times, and just tuck a few strawberries into that space, be careful as to which space you choose. The very presence of the aforementioned could carry verticillium wilt and root lice.

If, in the middle of enjoying someone else's strawberry crop, you have said to yourself, "Next year we should have our own," pick up the spade and start digging as soon as you get home. There are a couple of reasons for this sudden action. One is that if you dig the bed you will be forced into planting it, for what true gardener can stand to see tilled earth with nothing in it? More to the point, preparing the bed six months ahead will make for ideal soil conditions the following spring. Dig the bed in the fall, incorporating a lot of well-rooted manure into the soil, and either plant it with winter rye or just let it "season" over the winter. For strawberries, the pH should be on the acid side of the scale—5.5 to 6.0. The soil should be well composted, rich in organic matter and of the sandy-loam variety.

PLANTING

Site selection is extremely important when planting strawberries and the prime consideration is drainage. Nobody wants a soggy strawberry. A good eye test for drainage is to watch what happens to the site after a heavy rainfall. The puddles should disappear within an hour. As these plants bloom very early in the spring, they must not be in a frost pocket and since you may be told that the best site is a slope, don't forget that steep slopes can wash out. Slight slope? Fine.

When the plants arrive, check their state of health. If any show signs of winter injury—a black or brown discoloration in the plant crown or a heavy covering of mold—discard those plants; they probably will not survive anyhow. If you are not ready for their arrival—and are we ever?—put the plants in the refrigerator for a few days, keeping the roots moist.

There are various systems or designs for planting strawberries. This is where the going can get complicated because you have to allow for the offspring, or runners. The three possible systems are the matted row, the hill and the spaced runner. On paper they all look precise and decorative like needlepoint patterns. Once in the garden it is all a bit untidy, but you have to lay out some sort of planting plan and the matted row is the one most acceptable to home gardeners.

Space the rows 3½ to 4 feet apart and set plants 18 inches apart. The runners will form a mat 15 to 18 inches wide, making solid rows of green leaves with well-weeded soil between each row.

You have your bed, your plan and a cool day. Using a spade, dig down about 6 inches for the hole. Set the plant with the crown (the spot where the roots and stem join) as deep as it was before. The roots should be well spread out and the soil should cover only the base of the crown. Press the soil down firmly and water well. Remove all blossoms the first year. How many plants should you put in? As many as you have room for. For most people, there's no such thing as an overabundance of strawberries. A computer rule of thumb is: One hundred feet of plants divided between early- and late-producing will be enough for a family of five.

PLANTING STRAWBERRIES

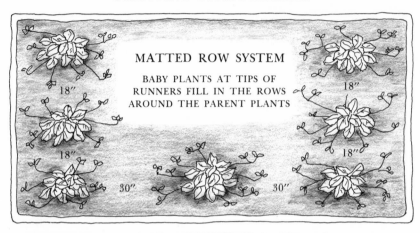

MATTED ROW SYSTEM

BABY PLANTS AT TIPS OF RUNNERS FILL IN THE ROWS AROUND THE PARENT PLANTS

18"

18"

18"

18"

30"

30"

SPACED RUNNER SYSTEM

RUNNER PLANTS ARE PLANTED TO GROW 4"-6" APART

4"-6"

4"-6"

4"-6"

4"-6"

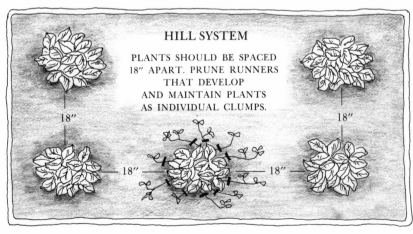

HILL SYSTEM

PLANTS SHOULD BE SPACED 18" APART. PRUNE RUNNERS THAT DEVELOP AND MAINTAIN PLANTS AS INDIVIDUAL CLUMPS.

18"

18"

18"

18"

MULCHING

Mulching is a good idea even in the warmer climates just to keep the berries clean. In cold areas a winter blanket of straw or hay is necessary. Put it on 3 to 4 inches deep after the first frost and pull it aside in the spring when growth starts.

FERTILIZING

Well-rotted manure placed in the soil before planting is the best possible start for these plants. After the first month or six weeks, if the plants look a bit pale and weak give them some nitrogen. Another dose of commercial fertilizer should be applied in the late summer. From then on, an established bed needs feeding only after the final harvest.

PRUNING AND RENEWING

You have removed the blossoms as you planted. Keep picking them off during the first growing season and cheer yourself up with dreams of the future. What's one year in a gardener's life?

No sloppy housekeeping is allowed in the strawberry bed. It should be kept free of weeds or you'll have a tangled mess, and the runners themselves can cause a problem. Given good soil and plenty of water, most plants will produce many runners the first season. But enough is enough; too many will just decrease yield and quality. Incidentally, this is why you have to dig up and replant every third year. The bed will become so matted that the plants just won't produce well. The best system is the one that allows the largest number of runners to root without crowding. This is the matted row system. Having put in your plants, let the runners root at random or space them 6 to 12 inches. (This is the extra hand labor you may not want to bother with but it does result in higher yields and better quality.) When the row is filled with plants to a width of 12 to 15 inches, start cutting off the runners as they form. The runners you get rooted early in the season are much more productive than the ones you root later on.

When it comes to plant renewal, this is where you realize that with strawberries you must work for your supper. The best year is the second year. After that the yield will drop off and it is time to replant. You can let the bed go a third year if you wish, but chances are the berries will be much smaller and fewer. Someone is sure to tell you that that didn't happen to him and he may be right; but it was luck.

There are various methods for renewing your crop. Basically the idea is to destroy the least productive plants and keep the better ones—survival of the fittest. In the fall after the last harvest—and this is an all-in-one-day job—clean out the bed. Throw away the old plants and put the good runner plants into flats. Then fertilize the bed with nitrogen, weed it clean, and replace the best plants. Mulch and let lie. This is the method that works best for us but you could also narrow the rows to a strip 8 to 10 inches wide and thin out the plants, leaving the healthy ones. You will undoubtedly work out your own system as you go along. Suffice it to say, it must be done.

INSECTS AND DISEASES

The prevalence of these problems and the way to control them depends on your geographical location. If you start out with certified plants from virus-free stock, however, you will lessen the possibility of trouble in this area. A preventive spray program can be followed and there are specific sprays for specific insects and diseases. It is advisable to get this information from your state extension service.

HARVESTING

Finally, we pick. Up and out early before the dew is off the leaves. Pick only those that are red all over with no white showing at the cap. Pick only enough for that day; you can always run out and get more. Pick the berry—don't pull it—and make sure the stem and cap stay on as long as possible. Leave the ones you are going to eat fairly soon at room temperature and refrigerate the rest. It goes without saying that the flavor is at its peak when the berry is not chilled. As I said earlier, we never wash strawberries. If they do have some dirt on them, I brush it off with a damp paper towel. A very elegant French lady once told me that she always washed her strawberries in Port wine. Just a suggestion.

VARIETIES

Your main choice is between the Everbearing and the June-bearing or One-crop. Everbearing sounds Utopian, but it does have its drawbacks, the main one being that these berries do not do well under the hot summer sun; they become flavorless and soft. Another drawback is that they are much more trouble to cultivate. Some experts say that they should be grown on raised beds, shaded from the afternoon sun and kept well watered all summer long. To me it is preferable to have one glorious crop when the season is right, eat strawberries until we've had our fill, and that's that until next year. The jam will be with us all winter and, made with perfectly ripe berries and no pectin, it is incomparably delicious. Culinary note: Just as fresh straw-berries are at their best at room temperature, so is the jam. If it must be refrigerated after opening, take the time to warm it before spreading it on your toast or croissant. The juices will fairly run and you'll think it's June in January.

You can stretch the season by planting a combination of early, mid-season and late varieties. There are so many that it would be pointless to list them all, and, here again, the variety should be adapted to the climatic conditions. It is nice to know that strawberries will grow in just about every state including Alaska.

RECIPES

Strawberry Scorched Cream

6 SERVINGS

4 cups strawberries, hulled
2 tablespoons kirsch
5 eggs, separated
⅓ cup sugar
2 cups rich milk
4 tablespoons sugar

If berries are small, leave them whole. If large, halve them. Put on bottom of 1½-quart baking dish as many berries as will fit in one layer. Sprinkle with kirsch. Beat yolks until light, gradually adding ⅓ cup sugar. Scald milk and pour over yolks while beating. Pour mixture into saucepan and cook over medium heat, stirring constantly, until thick and smooth. Cool for 1 to 2 hours. Pour custard over strawberries and cover with plastic wrap. Chill for 3 to 4 hours. Beat egg whites until stiff, but not dry, gradually adding 2 tablespoons sugar. Cover custard with meringue. Sprinkle remaining 2 tablespoons of sugar over top. Place under broiler, 3 inches from flame, to brown. Watch carefully as it will burn quickly.

Strawberries in Wine

6 SERVINGS

    4 cups strawberries, hulled
    1 cup sugar
    ¼ teaspoon cinnamon
    1 cup Claret
    1 tablespoon honey
    2 tablespoons brandy

Preheat oven to 300°. Put berries in shallow baking dish in one layer. Mix sugar with cinnamon and sprinkle over berries. Place in oven for 15 to 20 minutes, until sugar has melted and juice has come from berries. Pour off liquid into small saucepan. Pour Claret over berries and return to oven for 15 minutes. Heat liquid in saucepan, adding honey and brandy. Cook for about 10 minutes, until thick and syrupy. Before serving, pour over berries. Serve hot.

Strawberries Romanoff

6 SERVINGS

    4 cups strawberries, hulled
    2 tablespoons sugar
    1 cup heavy whipping cream
    2 cups vanilla ice cream, softened
    ¼ cup Cointreau or Curaçao
    2 tablespoons brandy

Place strawberries in bowl and sprinkle with sugar. Let stand a few hours at room temperature. Whip cream until stiff. Beat whipped cream, liqueur and brandy into ice cream. Fold berries into this mixture and serve at once.

Strawberry Cones

CONES

2 eggs
½ cup sugar
1 tablespoon cold water
⅔ cup flour

Preheat oven to 350°. Beat eggs and sugar together until thick and lemon-colored. This will take about 10 minutes with an electric beater. Beat in water and flour until smooth. On well-greased cookie sheets, drop spoonfuls of batter 2 inches apart to form circles about 4 inches in diameter. Bake for 12 minutes or until edges are light brown. Remove from sheet, one at a time, leaving remainder in oven while forming circles into cone shapes with hands. These become brittle very quickly once they are exposed to the air so work quickly. Keep in a tight container in the freezer until ready to fill.

FILLING

2 egg whites
Pinch of salt
6 tablespoons sugar
1 cup heavy whipping cream
3 tablespoons rum
1 tablespoon lemon juice
2 cups strawberries, crushed

Beat egg whites with salt, gradually adding ¼ cup sugar. Beat until stiff. Whip cream with remaining sugar until stiff. Stir rum and lemon juice into strawberries. Fold fruit and cream into meringue mixture. Freeze until ready to use.

To serve, fill cones with softened strawberry mousse and garnish with a fresh strawberry on top of each.

Note: the cone batter can also be used to make Fortune Cookies.

132

RASPBERRIES

We all have to have favorites or, as one armchair philosopher put it, all ice cream would be vanilla. My own favorite berry is the raspberry. Unfortunately, I've chosen one that is slowly disappearing from view in the open market. Fortunately, we can grow them with a minimum of care and attention. This was actually the first berry we planted when we moved to our present location, due to the kindness of our next-door neighbor. She was a delightful elderly lady, who had personally tended her many gardens in younger days. At this point in time her fading strength had forced her to restrict her attentions to caring for indoor plants and her raspberry patch. Early spring saw her out in the yard pruning the canes and cleaning the winter's debris from the ground around the bushes. She loved her raspberries and was eager to share them with any who felt the same way. This was our first mutual bond of neighborliness and we quickly accepted her offer to transplant several of the sucker plants to our property. They flourished and we have since added several more.

The word "patch" is picturesque but does suggest something a bit run down and ragged. This is not necessarily the way you should plant or keep your raspberries, although if you don't pay much attention to them they will go from ordered rows to a disordered patch very quickly. There is really nothing wrong with a patch but it is harder to clean out, prune and mulch, and eventually the quality of the berries will suffer.

As not too many people grow raspberries, we have found that they are truly a treat, and one of the nicest presents you can give your dinner hostess is a pint of fresh berries for her next morning's breakfast. Last summer we had a picnic by the sea and one friend, who has an old but well-tended patch, brought a cooler full of melon slices and raspberries, all to eat out of hand. A poetic combination of foods and one to keep in mind for your fall harvest when the melons are ripe and bursting with sunshine.

SOIL

The soil should have a lot of humus in it with possibly some sand mixed in. The dirt should be what we call "friable"— on the dry side, not caked together and pleasant to handle. Location is most important and, as with any flowering, fruiting plants, full sun is best. Like the strawberries, raspberries should not be planted where there have been any vegetables susceptible to wilt. Also, if there are any wild brambles near you, clean them; any diseases they might have will quickly spread. Next in order of importance comes drainage. Raspberries do not like to stand in puddles.

PLANTING

Dig by hand or rototill by machine the new bed a foot in depth and mix in some compost. By the way, rototilling is definitely a hard job. It is recommended that the raspberry bed be dug a year or six months in advance, covered with hay and allowed to set. We did not have time to do this as we moved early in the spring and had to put our gratuitous plants in immediately. Luckily, we have very good soil, the plants took hold and we have never had any trouble. You have to use your own judgment on this. If possible, let the freshly turned bed sit for a week or two. If your plants have arrived, leave them in a cool spot and do not let the roots dry out.

Plan to place the red raspberry bushes 2 feet apart in rows that are 4 feet apart. Black raspberry bushes go in 3 feet apart in rows 6 feet apart. Put the bush into the hole, setting the red raspberry 2 to 3 inches deeper than it was in the nursery. Spread the roots apart carefully. Cover the roots with dirt; fill the hole with soil and tamp it down firmly. Water well and cut the canes back to 3 inches from the ground. Plant the black raspberry at the same depth as it was in the nursery with the crown just below the ground. Cut the canes back to 3 inches.

MULCHING

The most important treatment you can give these berry bushes is a good layer of mulch 6 to 8 inches deep all around them. The mulch can be hay, sawdust, sugarcane, wood chips, or any organic material. This keeps the roots moist and also provides food for the plants.

FERTILIZING

Raspberry bushes really don't need any other feeding except a dressing of manure in the early spring just as the new growth begins.

PRUNING

Raspberry canes are biennial; they grow the first year (no fruit), produce the second year, and then die. The crown and roots are perennial and new canes grow from buds on the base of the old canes. In this way they are constantly replenishing themselves. After the canes have borne their fruit, cut them down 2 to 3 inches above the ground and remove most of the suckers. This seems like ruthless treatment but it will give the remaining canes air circulation and help them bear better later on. In the fall, prune the whole patch again. Come spring, clean it out, removing all the dead and weak canes and cutting the healthy survivors down to 3 inches. Really good housekeeping is the name of the game and it pays off in larger, better berries.

To get new plants from your old ones, just open your eyes and take a look at what's coming up around them. You can either mow down suckers or dig them up and replant for new bushes. That is the way to increase the red raspberries. The blackcaps have a slightly different method of propagating. They tend to go overland and the tips of their canes will root into the ground. In the fall, cover these tips with soil. Then in the spring, cut the newly rooted tips free from the parent plant, dig them up and replant where you want them. If you follow this cycle of birth and growth you will never be in need of raspberries.

INSECTS AND DISEASES

There will not be much of a problem with insects, and disease can be kept to a minimum if you choose disease-resistant varieties; plant in clean, healthy soil; remove old canes after harvest; cultivate assiduously, keeping the patch clean; destroy any plants that are diseased. Again, for specific problems that involve using pesticides, consult an authority.

HARVESTING

When the berries are a deep red and fall off in your hand when you touch them, it is time to pick them.

VARIETIES

Raspberries grow best in cool climates. They are not well suited to areas south of Virginia, Tennessee or Missouri, nor to states where the summers are hot and dry and winters are extremely cold. The key to choosing varieties is, of course, to choose one that produces best in your area and to buy certified stock. There are always new varieties being developed, such as the lyrically named Brandywine—a big, beautiful, lush berry that was shown to me at the New York State Fruit Testing Association by its proud father, Dr. Ourecky. This berry will be available to the homeowner soon and it is just one of many new types that we will have access to in the future. Do not plant black raspberries anywhere near the red as the blacks are susceptible to wilt, virus disease and rust and they will infect the red. The red raspberry is grown more extensively in the western states and the blackcaps seem to stick to the east and Oregon. Personally, we prefer the red over the black and so have stuck to them for the space we have available. It's a purely personal preference and you choose what you like.

RECIPES

Frozen Raspberry Cream

6 CUPS

⅔ cup sugar
⅓ cup water
¼ teaspoon cream of tartar
2 egg whites
1½ cups heavy cream
1½ cups fresh raspberries, slightly crushed

Combine sugar and water in a small saucepan and bring to a boil, stirring until sugar dissolves. Add cream of tartar; reduce heat to medium and cover pan. Boil until syrup spins a thread. Beat whites until foamy. Add syrup to whites, beating in 1 tablespoon at a time. Keep checking to see if syrup is still thread-like. If not, return to heat until it gets to that point again. When all syrup has been added, beat until mixture cools. Stir in cream and raspberries. Turn into container of ice-cream maker and freeze according to product directions. Serve with raspberry sauce made by blending raspberries into a puree. You may sieve out the seeds if you wish.

Note: A simple and delicious dessert can be made by layering the raspberry cream, blackberry sorbet (see page 145) and orange cream (see page 91) in a clear glass soufflé dish. Freeze and decorate with fresh strawberries before serving. It's a very good idea if you have a small amount left over from each recipe.

Russian Raspberry Pudding

4 SERVINGS

2 cups raspberries
1 cup sour cream
2 eggs
1 tablespoon sugar
1 tablespoon flour

Preheat oven to 350°. Place raspberries in a 3- to 4-cup deep baking dish. Place dish in oven for 10 minutes. Beat sour cream with eggs, sugar and flour. Pour sour cream mixture over raspberries. Bake for 40 to 45 minutes until firm and lightly browned. Serve warm or at room temperature.

Raspberry-Wineberry Jam

Raspberries
½ as many wineberries (if you have them)
Sugar
Water

Mash the fruit well and strain through a sieve. Throw away half the pulp remaining in the sieve and add the remaining half to the strained fruit. Measure amount of sugar: for each cup of strained fruit allow ⅔ cup of sugar. Measure the total amount of sugar and allow 1 cup water to each 5 cups sugar. Boil water and sugar together for 5 minutes to make a syrup. Add the strained fruit and boil, skimming constantly until it sheets from the spoon. Pour into sterilized jars and seal, following the Instructions for Preserving on page 185.

Jelly and jam making is not easy to give directions for as so much depends on the condition of the fruit and one person's idea of "sheeting" may not be another's. Just don't let it boil too long because a soft, runny jam is much preferable to a hard, rubbery jam.

Raspberry and currant is also a delicious combination.

Syllabub

4 CUPS

1 cup heavy cream
½ cup confectioners' sugar
2 egg whites
2 tablespoons cream sherry
2 cups fresh raspberries
½ cup slivered toasted almonds

Whip cream until stiff, gradually adding ¼ cup sugar. Beat egg whites until foamy. Continue beating while adding remaining sugar. Beat until stiff. Combine the two mixtures and stir in the sherry, blending well. Pour over raspberries. Garnish with slivered toasted almonds.

BLACKBERRIES

When we go out on the first warmish day—that glorious day when the wind no longer has sharp edges—and view the ravages of winter, it is hard to believe that those brownish-red canes will ever produce anything as truly beautiful as the blackberry. It is one of nature's ugly-duckling-into-swan miracles, and if you are one of the less fortunate who do not have wild blackberries growing near you, then you are missing a lot. We planted our blackberries after a trip to Ireland, where we saw miles of berry hedgerows in bloom, their starry flowers filling the air with a soft scent and the promise of fat ripe fruits that would be transformed into sugary deep-dish pies and cobblers, refreshing sorbets and small pots of orange-flavored jams.

Perhaps this is nothing new to you; you may have been spoiled all these years with a patch of these berries growing wild near your home. For those of us who have not been rewarded by nature in this bountiful manner, it is nice to know that blackberries will grow, generally speaking, in any part of the United States; that is, the bush, or erect, blackberry. The trailing blackberry must be protected during the winter in the northern climates.

This ancient berry is comparatively easy to grow and propagates by suckers and root cuttings. It has stout canes that do not need staking necessarily and stout thorns that can produce an impenetrable hedge. Gloves are essential when working with the blackberry bush, but personally I prefer the thorny to the thornless for a more flavorful product. There are some things in nature that are just not worth trying to change. The thorns may be troublesome but they do manage to keep out unwanted invaders, so think of that aspect when you decide on the location of your blackberry hedge.

These bushes do need to be kept in check as they have an unruly tendency to show up in unexpected places, but that is merely a matter of pruning. Among the bramble fruits, blackberries can be described as "dependable," and once you get them going and growing, they should produce for as long as 15 to 20 years. Just think of all the beautiful desserts in your future, including a spicy jam cake, richly iced with caramel, that could turn a bleak February day into a dream of summer.

SOIL

We have found that the best location for our blackberry bushes is in a row near the edge of our property. There they do not seem to bother any of the other plants and we do not object to creating a small problem for the visiting dogs and other animals. However, the most important factor to consider is soil moisture. These brambles need a great deal of wetness during their growing and ripening period, but not during their dormancy, so the area should have good drainage. Any good garden soil, except that which is very sandy, will do.

PLANTING

As with many of the berry patches, it is recommended that you prepare your soil a season ahead of your planting by plowing and sowing a green manure crop of something like rye, which adds organic matter and nitrogen to the soil. However, if this is not practical, prepare your soil as you would for any planting, digging down to a depth of 9 to 10 inches and making a good clean bed. Naturally, the addition of some good manure mixed in with the soil is desirable. Here again, there is danger of wilt if these berries are planted in soil that has previously contained potatoes, tomatoes, peppers or eggplant.

If you have a handyman handy, now's the time you need him. While blackberry bushes (the erect variety) can stand alone, support will help and reduce the problem of broken canes. Obviously the trailing variety depend on some kind of trellising. That word conjures up pictures of an elaborate building program, but without going all out to be decorative you can keep your blackberries very happy with some posts and wire. Set posts 15 to 20 feet apart in the row. String one wire between the posts about 2½ feet from the ground for the erect variety. For the trailing berries, use two wires—one 3 feet from the ground, the other 5 feet from the ground. Use soft string to tie the canes to the wires. Do not tie the canes in bundles.

After the bushes have been in a couple of years and are thriving, you may decide to be more decorative and turn your wires into split rails. This does make a most attractive fence arrangement, especially when the bushes are in full bloom, and if you do a small section at a time it is not such an overwhelming project.

MULCHING

Because these plants have shallow roots, mulching is a good answer. The mulching will protect the roots from weather damage and adds to clean cultivation.

FERTILIZING

If you want to do some feeding, and it is always a good idea, apply fertilizer at bloom time and again following the fruit harvest. Use a commercial 5-10-5 mixture for the first application and ammonium nitrate for the second feeding. Do this from the second year on.

PRUNING

The crowns of blackberry plants are perennial and their canes are biennial (they live for two years). During their first year the canes send out side branches called "laterals." Small branches grow from buds on these laterals during the second year and fruit is borne on these buds. After the laterals bear fruit, the canes die. So much for the growth pattern, but when you are told to prune at a specific time, it helps to know why. In the spring we prune the laterals back to about 12 inches in order to help the fruit growth.

Brambles like to bring in all the relatives and they are a most prolific family, so it is up to you to practice a bit of planned parenthood or you'll have Brer Rabbit's brier patch in no time. Remove all the suckers that come up between the rows. Do this by pulling them out of the ground. Did I mention gloves? Each year in the late winter when wandering restlessly around the garden, eager to get started on outdoor projects, I do a bit of pruning or pulling with bare hands. It only takes one good prick to remind me that no matter what the season the brambles keep their natural protection against the enemy.

When the canes of the erect blackberries grow to about 3 feet, cut off the tips and the canes will branch out. Then, after the last harvest, cut out all the old canes and thin the new canes to 3 or 4 for the erect type and about 8 for the trailing variety. For the dewberries and trailing blackberries, you can let the canes ramble around the first year they are planted. They may grow to 15 feet in length. The second year they should be trellised. We do not attempt this type of blackberry growing in our climate (southern New England), but if you wish to try them it is essential to cover the canes in the winter. You may cover them heavily with leaves or any other good mulch, but first inquire as to how much success your neighboring gardeners have had with the trailing berries before you put them in. They may be more trouble than they're worth and we find we're very happy with just plain upright blackberry bushes.

Cultivate carefully as these plants have shallow roots. Once again, mulching is a good answer for this.

INSECTS AND DISEASES

The scourge of the brambles is orange rust and it is easy to spot because, unlike many of the other plant diseases, it is most aptly named. It starts with a yellowish color appearing on the underside of the new leaves in the spring. This becomes bright orange during the summer. The disease is systemic, which means it travels throughout the plant, and any suckers will have it also. The only cure is to root out and burn all infected canes and you may have to do this several times throughout the season.

Double blossoms, another sickness, is just what its sounds like. Extra, somewhat deformed petals are formed in the spring from soft, reddish buds. These should be broken off and burned.

The two insects that attack blackberries are also enemies of the raspberry. The "Red-Necked Cane Borer" will cause cigar-shaped swellings near the base of the canes, and you must prune out the damaged canes and burn them. The "Raspberry Crown Borer" doesn't give any visible signs as to his presence until you take a careful look at the old canes after harvest. You will see some holes and a hollow area at ground level. If you decide that this situation is bad enough to warrant the use of herbicides, ask for professional advice.

HARVESTING

My only advice is: be patient. The berry should be black all over and fairly oozing its juices before it is picked. You must give it time to produce maximum sugar content.

VARIETIES

The blackberry that we hear the most about is Darrow, possibly because it is early, has a long fruiting season, is very productive and is a good, hardy plant. Bristol is another variety with the same qualities. Probably the most important feature of any of these is on the label: "Virus-Free." That little legend will save you many headaches and we are foolish not to take advantage of the intensive research that has been done by our experiment stations to make life easier for us.

Lucretia is a popular trailing variety that ripens early and is very productive. There are many others, including Logan and Boysen, so check the specialists in your area before ordering. If you're going to do it, do it right.

RECIPES

Blackberry Upsidedown Cake

6 SERVINGS

    2 tablespoons butter
    ¼ cup brown sugar
    2 cups blackberries
    1¾ cups sugar
    ½ cup butter or margarine
    2 eggs
    1½ cups flour
    2 teaspoons baking powder
    ½ teaspoon salt
    ½ cup milk
    1 teaspoon vanilla or fruit liqueur

Preheat oven to 350°. In an 8- or 9-inch round pan or iron skillet, heat butter and brown sugar over medium heat; add berries. Cook, stirring, until bubbling. Add ¾ cup sugar and crush berries slightly. Cook for 5 minutes. Remove from heat and set aside.

Cream butter and 1 cup sugar until light. Beat in eggs, one at a time, blending well. Mix together the flour, baking powder and salt and add alternately to creamed mixture with milk. Stir in vanilla or fruit liqueur. Pour batter over fruit in pan. Bake for 35 to 40 minutes until cake tests done. Let stand in pan until lukewarm. Run knife around edge of pan and turn out onto large plate. Serve with whipped cream.

Blackberry Sorbet

6 TO 8 SERVINGS

6 cups blackberries
½ cup sugar or to taste
2 tablespoons kirsch or crème de cassis
2 egg whites
2 tablespoons sugar

Puree blackberries in blender. Strain to remove seeds. Stir sugar and liqueur into berries. Turn into freezer tray or bowl and freeze about 1 hour until mushy. Remove from freezer and stir up. Beat egg whites with 2 tablespoons sugar until stiff. Fold into blackberry mixture and return to freezer for several hours. Remove from freezer about 10 minutes before serving. This is a very refreshing dessert. Serve with almond cookies.

Blackberry Jam

Blackberries
Sugar to taste
Grated rind of 1 orange
Juice of 1 orange

Press blackberries through a sieve. Discard half the seeds and add the remainder to the strained pulp. Measure pulp and allow ⅔ cup of sugar for each cup of pulp. Put pulp, sugar, orange juice and rind in kettle and bring to a boil. Boil until thick and jam sheets from spoon. Skim frequently. Pour into sterilized jars and seal, following the Instructions for Preserving on page 185.

Blackberry Jam Cake

1 cup butter or margarine
1 cup granulated sugar
1 cup brown sugar
5 eggs, separated
3 cups flour
1 teaspoon baking soda
1 teaspoon cinnamon
1 teaspoon mace
½ teaspoon allspice
1 cup buttermilk
½ cup chopped dates
½ cup chopped walnuts
1 cup blackberry jam (see page 145)

Preheat oven to 350°. Cream together the butter and sugars until very light, beating for about 10 minutes. Mixture should be almost white in color and the consistency of whipped cream. Beat in the egg yolks. In a separate bowl, mix together the flour, soda, cinnamon, mace and allspice. Beat into the first mixture alternately with buttermilk. Stir in dates, nuts and jam. Mix well. Beat whites until stiff but not dry and fold in gently. Turn into 2 well-greased and floured 9-inch cake tins. Bake for 35 to 40 minutes until cake tests done in center. Let stand for 5 minutes. Turn out onto racks to cool. When cool, fill and frost with caramel icing.

CARAMEL ICING

1 cup sugar	½ cup butter
1 cup brown sugar	⅔ cup heavy cream

146

Put all ingredients in large saucepan. Boil for almost 10 minutes until mixture reaches soft ball stage (234°). Cool. Beat until thick enough to spread.

Blackberry Roll

6 SERVINGS

4 cups blackberries
1 cup white sugar
1 cup brown sugar
2 cups flour
3 teaspoons baking powder
½ teaspoon salt
6 tablespoons butter or margarine
⅔ cup buttermilk

Preheat oven to 375°. Put blackberries in bowl with sugars. Toss gently and let stand. In a large bowl, mix the flour, baking powder and salt. Cut in 4 tablespoons butter until mixture resembles coarse crumbs. Add buttermilk slowly until dough is soft but no longer sticky. Roll out dough to ½-inch thickness in a rectangular shape. Spread with sugar-soaked berries. Dot with remaining 2 tablespoons butter. Roll up, starting on the long side. Put roll in lightly greased baking pan, put any remaining berries along the sides of the roll. Bake for 30 minutes, basting with juice and berries. Roll should be well glazed with juice. Serve warm with hard sauce.

HARD SAUCE

1 cup butter
½ cup sugar
Brandy to taste

Beat butter and sugar together until very smooth and well blended. Add brandy slowly.

147

BLUEBERRIES

Is there another fruit that has inspired so many picturesquely named desserts as the blueberry? We have, to name but a few, flummery, buckle, duff, fool, slump and grunt. We also have the more commonplace tart, cake, pudding, muffin, pancake, turnover and pie. As a matter of fact, the fruit itself is blessed with more colloquial names than any other, being referred to variously as the whortleberry, hurtleberry, whin berry, blaeberry, trackleberry and bilberry. Any of these will do, but please, not huckleberry. The old-timers could tell which was which simply by biting the berry. The seeds of the blue are soft and not noticeable; those of the huckleberry are ten in number, large in size and bony in texture.

While we may feel that the blueberry has been with us forever—and it has in its wild state—the cultivated blue is a comparative newcomer to the garden scene. Although each area of the country had its wild blueberry, these bushes resisted any attempt to be transplanted, clinging stubbornly to that acid, sandy soil which answered all of their nutritional requirements. It wasn't until early in this century that botanists began to seriously study what it would take to make the blue thrive in upland conditions, as opposed to its native swampy area. The answer, as we all now know, is acid soil. Blueberries are related to the cranberry, rhododendron, azalea and laurel; where they grow, so grows the blueberry.

If you never thought seriously about pH before, you must do so now; that is, if you want the fun of popping fat, ripe clusters of blueblack berries off a bush and into a pudding sweetened with maple sugar; or a pie spiced with lemon and a whiff of cinnamon; or a bread shiny with a sugared orange crust; or enormous feathery pancakes layered with berries stewed in a juniper-lemon sauce. It is the promise of these epicurean delights that will make you till the soil a little harder to come up with the perfect pH for your blueberry bushes. And what is that perfect condition? The magic number is 4.5, and anything between 4.0 and 5.0 will do with little modification.

You may now ask, why should I go to all this trouble about soil if I can buy cultivated blueberries in my market all summer? Right. That gives you the berries but not the bush, and if we can get away from food for the stomach for a moment and think about food for the soul, a blueberry bush is a beautiful thing to behold in any of its growing seasons, with clusters of berries among the glossy green leaves in summer that change to the fiery flames of fall as the season comes to a close. They are a very decorative item and deserve more than just being set in a row somewhere on the property. Think about a hedge, perhaps edging the driveway or terrace, or a fence leading up to the kitchen door. And there we are, eating again. But the blueberries *are* the best of both worlds.

SOIL

A sandy soil with a pH of 4.5 is best but more than any of us can probably expect without helping nature along a bit. If you have heavier common garden soil, you can lighten it by digging in some sand and make it more acid with the addition of peat moss or sawdust. Very finely ground sulfur or ammonium sulfate may be used to increase acidity or you may add peat moss, mixing it with the garden soil, one part soil to one part peat by volume. This treatment not only helps the soil-content acidity but helps improve aeration and water-holding capacity. Blueberry plants have fine and fibrous roots and while they like water they must have good drainage.

As is true for many other berry plantings, it is best to prepare the soil at least a season ahead to get rid of weeds and thoroughly incorporate the fertilizer into the soil. If you don't have time to think this far in advance, then dig your bed and prepare the soil using $\frac{1}{3}$ loam, $\frac{1}{3}$ sand and $\frac{1}{3}$ peat moss. (By now you must realize that you're going to buy a lot of peat to keep the blueberries happy.) Mix in some complete fertilizer, such as 10-10-10, being sure to blend it all thoroughly to prevent damage to the plant roots.

149

PLANTING

Set the plants out in early spring as soon as the soil can be worked. Dig your holes and set the bushes 1 to 2 inches deeper than they were in the nursery. Place them 4 to 8 feet apart in rows 8 to 10 feet apart. These are recommended distances. We have ours closer together and they do very well, but this is the individual leeway we are all allowed in gardening. Just make sure the roots are not crowded. After setting in the plants, fill the hole 3/4 full of soil and water it. Then fill the hole and tamp down firmly.

MULCHING

Mulching is very important for these bushes and those who know recommend sawdust first, peat moss second; then there is hay, pine needles or wood shavings. About 6 inches of mulch is satisfactory and should be reapplied often enough to keep the level up. Having been through a long drought period here in New England some years ago, we learned our lesson on mulching and would never do without it again. In addition to helping the water situation it helps the maintenance problems, and the less weeding, the better.

FERTILIZING

Nitrogen is most important here and can be furnished by applying ammonium sulfate, but if you are putting on peat moss as a mulch, it should do the job without any extra fertilizer needed. There are signs, such as the condition and color of the leaves, that will tell you the plant's needs. Nothing works perfectly and we all go through those periods of wondering what is the matter with this tree, that bush, those vegetables. Sometimes it's just a bad year for that particular plant but it keeps us from being too complacent.

PRUNING

Start pruning right away by removing all weak growth from the new plants. Also take off all the large flower buds the first year; they will prevent fruiting. Pruning is done every spring as soon as the buds begin to swell and you can pick out the fruit buds from the small leaf buds.

To get the best production from the bushes, it is advisable to remove excess fruit buds. Take off the less vigorous twiglike canes, cutting them back to a strong lateral branch. On the strong canes, remove about half of the fruit buds and prune the weaker of the new growth. You cannot expect a really full crop of berries until the fourth year, assuming you put in two-year-old bushes.

Here are three simple rules to follow for pruning as set down by Stiles and Bailery in an article on growing blueberries:

- Remove sucker shoots and weak branches.
- Allow one fruit bud for each 3 inches of new shoot growth.
- Allow a maximum of 6 to 8 canes for old bushes.

INSECTS AND DISEASES

It is generally conceded that birds get first prize at being the enemy of the blueberry. There is no other solution but to net the crop. We have found one of the best nettings to use is fishnet. Rather than just tossing it lightly over the bushes, you really should build a frame and secure the net tightly to it.

We have never had a problem with insects but they do exist—the beetle, apple maggot, plum curculio and fruit fly. However, if you keep a clean bed and do regular pruning, these pests should leave you alone. The same rules apply to preventing disease. Healthy stock that is planted properly and well cared for seldom gets sick.

HARVESTING

There is really quite a long season for blueberries and it can extend over six weeks, so my only advice is not to get too impatient. Wait until the berry is completely blue, actually verging on black or purple, before picking. If there is a hint of greenish-white near the stem, leave it on the bush. Like other fruits, the berries should almost drop off when ready.

VARIETIES

Point one: Grow more than one kind as they are self-sterile. Point two: Stretch out your season by planting early, mid-season and late varieties. Point three: Start with two-year-old plants.

At one time it was not possible to maintain blueberry bushes in the warmer or southern areas. The only cultivated blue available was the highbush, and that had to have frequent cold nights. Now we have a delightfully named variety, the Rabbiteye, just suited for southern climes. Although it is a lowbush, the name apparently comes from the resemblance of the berry to a rabbit's eye, not the fact that the bush is as high as. . . . Some of the well-known varieties of highbush are Earliblue, Bluehaven, Darrow, Lateblue, Bluecrop, Jersey and Coville. Some of the names for the Rabbiteye are Woodard, Southland, Briteblue, Tifblue and Homebell. The better catalogs or nurseries will tell you which bear when.

RECIPES

Blueberry Gin Sauce

3 CUPS

Grated rind of 1 large lemon
½ cup sugar
1 cup water
2 teaspoons cornstarch
2 cups fresh blueberries
3 tablespoons gin

Combine lemon rind, sugar and water in small saucepan. Bring to a boil, stirring until sugar is dissolved. Lower heat and simmer uncovered for 10 minutes. Strain and return syrup to saucepan. Dissolve cornstarch in 1 tablespoon cold water, stir in cornstarch mixture and cook over medium heat until thick. Add berries and cook for 10 minutes. Stir in gin. Cool and serve over lemon sherbet. Will keep 3 to 4 days.

Blueberry Orange Bread

2 tablespoons butter or margarine
1/4 cup boiling water
1/2 cup orange juice
Grated rind of 1/2 orange
1 egg
1 cup sugar
2 cups flour
1 teaspoon baking powder
1/4 teaspoon baking soda
1/2 teaspoon salt
1 cup blueberries
2 tablespoons lemon juice
2 tablespoons honey
1 tablespoon grated lemon rind

Preheat oven to 325°. Melt butter in boiling water in small bowl. Stir in orange juice and rind. In another bowl, beat egg with sugar until light. Mix together the flour, baking powder, baking soda and salt and add alternately with orange juice mixture to egg mixture. Beat until smooth. Fold in berries. Turn into a large 9 x 5 x 3-inch loaf pan or 2 smaller loaf pans. Bake for 1 hour and 10 minutes until firm and golden. Turn out on rack placed over waxed paper. Mix together the lemon juice, honey and lemon rind. Spoon over hot loaf to glaze. Do not slice until cold. Spread with sweet butter or cream cheese.

Blueberry Crunch

This is terribly rich but you must make it once during the blueberry season.

6 SERVINGS

> 1 cup oatmeal
> 1 cup brown sugar
> ½ cup flour
> ½ cup dry milk
> ½ teaspoon salt
> ½ teaspoon cinnamon
> ½ cup butter
> 1½ cups blueberries

Preheat oven to 350°. In a large bowl, combine oatmeal, brown sugar, flour, dry milk, salt and cinnamon. Mix together. Cut in butter until mixture is crumbly. Spread about ⅔ of mixture in bottom of greased 8 x 8-inch baking dish. Spread blueberries over mixture. Top with remaining crumbs. Bake for 45 minutes until bubbling. Serve warm with homemade vanilla ice cream.

Cold Blueberry Soup

6 SERVINGS

> 2 cups blueberries
> 2 cups cranberry-apple juice
> Lemon yogurt to garnish

Place berries and juice into blender container. Blend until smooth. Chill for 3 to 4 hours. Serve with a spoonful of yogurt in each bowl.

Note: Strain the soup before serving if you wish.

Steamed Blueberry Pudding

6 SERVINGS

½ cup butter
½ cup sugar
1 egg
1½ cups flour
2 teaspoons baking powder
½ teaspoon salt
½ cup milk
Grated rind of ½ lime
1 cup blueberries

Cream together the butter and sugar until light. Beat in egg. Combine flour, baking powder and salt and add alternately with milk to creamed mixture. Stir in lemon rind. Fold in blueberries and turn batter into greased 1-quart mold or bowl. Place on rack in large saucepan and add boiling water to come halfway up side of mold. Cover saucepan and steam pudding 1 hour. Unmold and serve hot with lemon sauce or hard sauce.

LEMON SAUCE

Rind of 1 lemon, grated
Juice of 1 lemon
¼ cup sherry
⅓ cup sugar
2 eggs, separated

In top of double boiler, put all ingredients except egg whites. Set over hot water on medium heat and beat until thick. Beat whites until stiff and fold in. Serve warm.

Margaret Chase Smith's Blueberry Cake

½ cup butter or margarine
1 cup sugar
2 eggs
2 cups sifted flour
4 teaspoons baking powder
½ teaspoon salt
1 teaspoon grated nutmeg
1 cup milk
2 cups blueberries

Preheat oven to 375°. Cream shortening with sugar until light and creamy. Add eggs and beat well. Mix together the flour, baking powder, salt and nutmeg and add alternately with milk to creamed mixture. Fold in blueberries. Turn into 2 well-greased and floured 9-inch layer cake tins. Bake for 25 to 30 minutes. Let cake stand for 10 minutes. Turn out onto racks to cool. Put together and frost with a standard confectioners' sugar icing flavored with lemon to taste.

Blueberry Buckle

6 SERVINGS

½ cup butter or margarine
½ cup sugar
1 egg
2 cups flour
½ teaspoon salt
2½ teaspoons baking powder
½ cup sour cream
2 cups blueberries
½ cup sugar
½ cup flour
⅓ cup butter
½ teaspoon cinnamon

Preheat oven to 375°. Cream shortening and sugar until light. Beat in egg. Combine flour, salt and baking powder and add alternately with sour cream to creamed mixture. Spread dough in greased 9 x 9-inch pan. Spread blueberries on top of dough. Combine together until crumbly the sugar, flour, butter and cinnamon. Sprinkle over berries. Bake for 35 to 45 minutes until done.

Blueberry Pancake Pie

4 TO 5 SERVINGS

PANCAKE

1 cup flour
1 egg
2 tablespoons sugar
1½ tablespoons baking powder
½ cup buttermilk
½ teaspoon salt
½ cup melted butter

FILLING

Maple or brown sugar
Melted butter
Blueberry sauce (see page 158)

Combine all the pancake ingredients in large bowl and mix well. Heat a griddle and lightly grease it. Drop a large spoonful of batter onto hot griddle, spreading it out to make a 7-inch circle. Cook until brown on one side, turn and cook on other side. Remove to ovenproof serving dish. Sprinkle with maple or brown sugar, melted butter, and cover with blueberry sauce. Repeat, making 3 layers in all. Sprinkle maple sugar over top and glaze under broiler 3 inches from flame until bubbly. To serve, cut in wedge-shaped pieces.

BLUEBERRY SAUCE

⅓ cup sugar
1 tablespoon cornstarch
½ teaspoon salt
1 tablespoon lemon juice
¼ cup hot water
1 cup blueberries
2 teaspoons butter
2 tablespoons rum (optional)

Mix sugar, cornstarch and salt in small saucepan. Gradually stir in lemon juice and water. Cook and stir over medium heat until sauce becomes smooth and thickens. Stir in berries and cook, stirring, until sauce is thick. Remove from heat and stir in butter and rum.

GOOSEBERRIES AND CURRANTS

Gooseberry and gorse—tarts for tea and currant sauce with game; these are fruits right out of the pages of Thomas Hardy and Jane Austen and, unfortunately for the inveterate fruit lover, that is where they have stayed for many years. One English writer said, "Most Americans will never know the glory of the gooseberry as it is known in England." He goes on to note that the reason for this is that these fruits "languish" in hot weather. However, while it is true that currants and gooseberries are hardy enough to grow as far north as the Arctic Circle, it does not follow that they won't do well in this country in our middle and northern states. The *English* varieties don't do well, but we have some American varieties that manage very well indeed and become very sweet on the vine as well.

Actually, the main deterrent up to now in growing these two plants here has been a threat of disease; not a disease that harms the plants themselves but a disease that they carry, which can wipe out white pines anywhere near them. The spores can be wind-borne to a distance of 1,000 feet. This disease is called "white pine blister" and, while it is pretty much under control, there are still a few states that will not allow the importation of currants and gooseberries. However, any reputable nursery will warn you of this and will not sell you the plant if you live in one of these states. Your local extension service can always advise you on this too.

Neither of these neglected fruits lends itself to machine picking and they don't ship well so if you wish to experiment with a gooseberry fool or make jars of pure ruby red currant jelly to spread on hot buttered scones, investigate the possibility of planting a few of these hardy bush fruits.

Aside from their decorative and culinary features, these bushes have another advantage to the homeowner. You know that spot on the north side of the house that is a bit windswept and shaded for part of the day? You'd like to have planting there and you would really prefer a food-bearing type of bush. Well, here you have it and why hasn't anyone ever told you that not every fruit bush needs full sun? These not only don't need it, they can't take it. Furthermore, they are neat and tidy in their habits, not rambling all over the place, so they would fit nicely into a contained landscape plan. You probably wouldn't want too many, just enough for one tart, some jelly, a sauce or two, and perhaps a lovely English sweet called a tansy.

SOIL

Being heavy feeders, it stands to reason that these berries thrive on rich soil—strong clay loam, well endowed with compost, including wood ash and bonemeal. Their roots are near the surface and can be burned in a light sandy soil. Actually, they do best in the English type of climate, that misty cool air that is supposedly responsible for the famous English complexion. Approximate those conditions or compensate for them, and you'll have the answer.

PLANTING

"High on a windy hill" is to be taken literally here. Pick a northerly site where the bushes get the breezes; they like a lot of air. Both of these berries have something in common with clothes in a damp closet—they mildew if confined in an airless spot. You might take advantage of this feature and use these plants as a windbreak to protect other plants that are in an exposed area. Having also noted that the berries like partial shade, especially where summers are hot, just don't make it a corner where circulation is cut off. Set them out from the house. An ideal spot would be under the grape arbor where the light is filtered and they will avoid the intense noonday sun.

Because currants and gooseberries are ready for spring long before you are—they can even flower in the snow—it is a good idea to plant them in the fall or very early spring. Fall is feasible because they lose their leaves very early and go into dormancy well before other plants. This means that the root system becomes well developed before deep cold sets in.

Space plants about 5 feet apart, either in a row or an ornamental clump, putting them down a bit deeper than they were in the nursery. Tamp the soil down firmly. Remove any weak or broken shoots and trim remaining branches back to about 8 inches.

MULCHING

Since they are good feeders and have a shallow root system, you can undoubtedly guess that the best care you can give these berries is through mulching. The mulch should extend out to the tips of the roots, but leave a 6-inch circle around the base of the plant to discourage the field mice, who like nothing better than to nest and nibble.

FERTILIZING

When you are feeding the raspberries and blackberries in the early spring, just be sure to turn the corner to the north side of the house where it still feels like winter and give the currants and gooseberries a goodly amount of manure or 5-10-5. The spring rains or late winter snows will carry it down to the root systems.

PRUNING

The rule for pruning here is more like that for trees than for berries; that is, you want openness and good air circulation at the top. Do your pruning in early winter or very early spring. Sometimes in Europe, where they tend to be more deliberately decorative with their planting, you will see gooseberry bushes trimmed to form small trees. You might try this if you've an extra bush around to experiment with.

Gooseberry canes will fruit for about 3 years before losing vigor. The fourth year they should be cut to the ground. For a well-balanced bush, leave 3 to 4 branches the first year and 3 to 4 branches each year thereafter. This also applies to the currants; just remember that the gooseberry fruit bud produces 1 or 2 berries, the currant fruit bud produces a cluster.

Occasionally a gooseberry bush will reproduce itself by rooting one of its low-lying branches. To prevent this, cut out these laterals. However, this is one way of getting more bushes if you want them. Just bend over a low branch and bury the main part of it in the ground, letting the tip stick out. The buried section will root and a year later you can cut off the branch, dig up the rooted section and transplant it. Presto! More gooseberries.

INSECTS AND DISEASES

As you may have realized, one of the main problems with these bushes of English heritage is mildew, but that will only come about if your location warrants it. And you can buy mildew-resistant bushes now. "Anthracnose" could also be a problem, as could "mosaics." Pests in the form of cane borers and aphids are more of a nuisance than a real threat.

161

Generally speaking, these fruit bushes will not give you much to worry about. With proper cultivation, mulching and pruning they tend to take care of their own good health.

HARVESTING

Gooseberries are associated with gorse for a very good reason. They are thorny and not to be picked without gloves. When you pick them, the stems and petals will stay on the berry. Be sure to remove these before putting the berries into the pie. This is called "topping and tailing." A very neat way of harvesting currants was suggested by an old-time fruit gardener. When the berries are dead ripe, strip them from their stems with a table fork. He adds, "slightly crushed and liberally dusted with powdered sugar, allowed to stand for several hours in a refrigerator . . . they make a delicious supper dessert."

Gooseberries will ripen on the vine and, unless you are using them for jam, they are really much sweeter and tastier when ripe. Depending on the variety, they will be either a whitish green or pink.

Currants should be picked slightly underripe for jam or jelly because that is when the pectin content is the highest. Incidentally, it is not necessary to use commercial pectin in fruit jellies. I haven't yet found a fruit that wouldn't jell after a period of rapid boiling, be it long or short.

VARIETIES

Insure your investment by buying good stock from a good source. The American varieties of gooseberry will do better than the English, including the Pixwell, which is now practically thornless and turns pink when ripe, the Red Jacket, which produces large red-skinned berries and the Welcome, which is medium sized, red and mildew-resistant.

You'll find currants in three colors—black, red and white. Personally, I prefer the red and for that variety you could get either Red Lake or Minnesota 71.

RECIPES

Mary Norwak's Gooseberry Tansy

4 SERVINGS

½ cup butter
2 cups gooseberries, topped and tailed
2 egg yolks, beaten
½ cup heavy cream, lightly whipped
½ cup sugar
Juice of 1 lemon

Heat butter in skillet and simmer berries uncovered until soft. Stir in egg yolks and cream. Add sugar and cook gently until thickened slightly. Turn into serving dish and sprinkle with lemon juice and additional sugar to taste. Serve warm or cold.

Gooseberry Fool

6 SERVINGS

4 cups gooseberries, topped and tailed
6 tablespoons butter
1 cup sugar or to taste
2 cups heavy cream

Put gooseberries in heavy saucepan. Add butter in small pieces and heat slowly, stirring. When butter is melted, cover pan and stew berries for about 10 minutes until soft. Stir in sugar to taste. Cool for 3 to 4 hours.

Whip cream until stiff and fold in gooseberry mixture. Turn into large glass bowl and chill.

Ruth Matson's Spiced Gooseberries

ABOUT 3 PINTS

8 cups gooseberries, topped and tailed
4½ cups brown sugar
1 cup cider vinegar
1 stick cinnamon, 2 inches long
8 whole cloves
¼ teaspoon ground nutmeg
2 whole allspice
½ cup water

Put sugar, vinegar and spices in large saucepan with ½ cup water and boil for 5 minutes. Add gooseberries and simmer covered about 30 to 40 minutes. When tender and syrup is thick, pour into sterile jars and seal, following the Instructions for Preserving on page 185.

Summer Pudding

4 SERVINGS

2 cups currants
½ cup sugar or more to taste
8 slices bread, crusts removed
1 tablespoon flour
6 tablespoons sugar
½ teaspoon salt
3 egg yolks
1½ cups milk
1 teaspoon vanilla
½ cup heavy whipping cream

Place currants and sugar in saucepan and cook gently until fruit is soft. Taste for sweetening. Line a 1-quart bowl or mold with bread slices, cut to fit. Reserve 2 slices for the top. Fill bowl with fruit and juice and cover with remaining bread slices. Cover with a saucer and weight down with heavy cans. Set in refrigerator overnight. In heavy saucepan, stir together the flour, sugar and salt. Mix in egg yolks and milk, whisking all together. Cook over medium heat, stirring constantly, until slightly thick and smooth. Do not boil. Strain into bowl and cover with plastic wrap. Cool and stir in vanilla. Chill for 4 to 5 hours. Whip cream until stiff and fold into custard. When ready to serve, unmold pudding onto serving platter and pour over some of the custard. Pass remaining custard in separate bowl.

Red Currant Jelly

3 CUPS

> 6 cups currants, washed and stemmed
> ½ cup water
> Sugar

Put currants and water in saucepan and boil gently for about 10 minutes until currants are soft and juicy. Put mixture into cheesecloth or jelly bags to drain. Do not squeeze. Measure juice and pour into saucepan. Bring to a boil and skim. Add an equal amount of sugar. Cook, skimming and stirring constantly until jelly sheets from side of spoon. Pour into sterilized glasses and seal, following the Instructions for Preserving on page 185.

Note: If you don't have time to make the jelly, you can freeze the juice and make it later.

Melba Sauce

2 CUPS

> 6 cups currants, washed and stemmed
> ½ cup water
> 1 cup raspberries, sieved
> ½ cup sugar
> 1 tablespoon cornstarch
> ½ teaspoon salt
> Sherry or Framboise to taste   *(continued)*

Put currants and water in saucepan and boil gently for about 10 minutes until currants are soft and juicy. In top of double boiler, put currant juice and raspberries. Mix together the sugar, cornstarch and salt and stir into fruit. Place over simmering water and cook until thick, stirring. Remove from heat, cool and flavor with sherry or liqueur to taste.

Note: Generally when sweetening fruit, it must be done according to taste.

Use this sauce over poached peaches, broiled bananas, peach or banana ice cream. Keeps for 3 to 4 days.

Pilgrim Lamb Stew

4 TO 5 SERVINGS

3 tablespoons butter
1 tablespoon oil
1 onion, chopped
2 pounds lamb for stew, well trimmed
Salt to taste
Freshly ground black pepper to taste
2 cups tomato catsup
½ cup currant jelly (see page 165)
¼ cup Madeira
Juice of 1 lemon

In large skillet, heat butter and oil. Sauté onion until soft. Add lamb and sauté until browned on all sides. Sprinkle with salt and pepper. In small saucepan, combine catsup, jelly, Madeira and lemon juice. Bring to a boil, stirring, and cook until jelly dissolves. Pour over meat in skillet. Cover and simmer for 1½ hours until meat is tender and sauce is thick and dark. Serve with fresh green beans and sautéed mushroom caps.

CHAPTER 6

RHUBARB

Surely the plants sing their songs of spring as clearly as the birds do, to those of us who are watching and waiting for the first signs of that soaring season. And who is more aware of those signs than the gardener to whom winter has been a period of fence mending and patient perusal of the seed catalogs?

Spring's "first herald" must certainly be the rhubarb plant, boldly poking its crinkled purple leaves through the still cold earth. As this shy season takes her own sweet time in putting in an appearance, there doesn't seem to be much we can do to hurry things along—with one exception. We *can* force the rhubarb and have our soothing sherbet, spicy cobblers, sauces and pies that much sooner.

Forcing is a very simple process really and I am surprised

167

more people don't take advantage of this method to get a head start on the seasonal fruits. Just take a box or barrel, about 18 inches high, and knock out both ends. Set it over the plant; the tender stalks will reach onwards and upwards, ready for picking that much sooner. These stalks will be pinker in color and less tough than those left to mature on their own.

Though the large green leaves are poisonous, containing oxalic acid, they are handsome and decorative enough to be border plants or to set against a stone wall or wooden fence. They need full sun, but for only half of the day, so you could use rhubarb as a splendid focal point in your overall landscaping plan. I suppose a thrifty New Englander would nod his head and say, "Yep, can't beat that. You can eat it and admire it too." And he's right. Another thrifty note: Don't buy rhubarb plants. Beg them from a neighbor.

Rhubarb likes heavily fertilized, moist soil and should be planted early in the spring. Set the plants in the ground about 3 feet apart with the bud just 2 inches below the surface of the soil. Mulch it well and leave it until the next spring when it will be ready for cutting. Mulch heavily in the fall and fertilize in the spring. Rhubarb should be thinned or divided every 6 to 7 years and this is the time when you can be generous with your neighbors. Dig it up before the leaves uncurl. Wash away the soil so you can see the roots. Cut them into sections and leave one bud on each division. Then just replant, starting the cycle all over again. This is one of the easiest plants to take care of and its rewards are great.

If you do buy your roots, Victoria, Valentine and Canada Red are all good, reliable strains but, if possible, take what your friends have to offer and don't worry about names.

RECIPES

Sour Cream Rhubarb Squares

8 SQUARES

½ cup sugar
½ cup chopped walnuts
2 tablespoons melted butter
1 teaspoon cinnamon
¼ teaspoon ginger
Grated rind of 1 lemon
1½ cups brown sugar
½ cup butter or margarine
1 egg
2 cups flour
1 teaspoon baking soda
⅛ teaspoon salt
1 cup sour cream
1½ cups rhubarb, cut into ½-inch pieces

Preheat oven to 350°. In small bowl, mix together the sugar, nuts, butter, cinnamon, ginger and lemon rind until crumbly. Set aside. Cream together the brown sugar and shortening until very light. Beat in the egg. In another bowl, stir together the flour, baking soda and salt and add to creamed mixture alternately with sour cream. Stir in rhubarb. Turn into greased and floured 9 x 9-inch pan. Sprinkle nut mixture over top. Bake for 45 to 50 minutes until cake tests done in center. Cut into squares and serve warm with whipped cream or ice cream.

Pork Roast with Rhubarb Sauce

6 SERVINGS

> 1 pork loin (4 pounds)
> Salt to taste
> Freshly ground black pepper to taste
> 2 cups rhubarb, cut into ½-inch pieces
> 2 tablespoons honey
> 2 tablespoons brown sugar
> ¼ cup chicken bouillon
> ¼ teaspoon salt
> 1 teaspoon cinnamon
> 1 tablespoon finely chopped fresh ginger root or 1 teaspoon ground ginger

Preheat oven to 325°. Sprinkle pork with salt and pepper and put on rack in baking pan. Roast for 30 minutes. Place rhubarb in heavy saucepan with honey, brown sugar, bouillon and salt. Bring to a boil, stirring. Turn heat to simmer and cook uncovered until rhubarb is soft and mixture is thick. Stir in spices. Spread top of pork roast with rhubarb mixture. Continue to roast for 1½ hours, adding more rhubarb sauce if necessary. To serve, carve into slices and pour sauce over each slice.

Rhubarb Sherbet

6 SERVINGS

> 4 cups rhubarb, cut into ½-inch pieces
> 1 cup sugar
> ½ cup light corn syrup
> ½ cup orange juice
> 2 tablespoons lemon juice
> Grated rind of 1 orange
> 2 egg whites
> Pinch of salt
> 2 tablespoons sugar

Place rhubarb in large saucepan with sugar, corn syrup, juices and orange rind. Cover, bring to a boil, then lower heat and stew until rhubarb is tender, about 10 minutes. Pour mixture into a bowl and let cool. Put bowl into freezer and let freeze until of a mushy consistency, from 1 to 2 hours, depending upon your freezer. Beat mixture until light and frothy. Beat egg whites with salt, gradually adding sugar until stiff. Fold into rhubarb mixture and return to freezer. Let solidify for several hours, stirring occasionally. Serve with ginger cookies.

Rhubarb Cheese Pie

8 SERVINGS

Pastry for one 10-inch piecrust
1 cup sugar
3 tablespoons cornstarch
4 cups rhubarb, diced in ½-inch pieces
4 packages (3 ounces each) cream cheese, softened
2 eggs
Grated rind of 1 lemon
1 cup sour cream
½ cup slivered almonds

Preheat oven to 425°. Roll out piecrust and place in pie pan. In saucepan, mix ½ cup sugar and cornstarch. Add rhubarb and cook, stirring until thickened and tender. Pour into pie shell and bake for 10 minutes. In bowl, beat cream cheese, eggs, remaining sugar and lemon rind together. Pour over rhubarb. Reduce oven temperature to 350°. Return pie to oven and bake for 30 minutes until set. Remove from oven, spread with sour cream, and return to oven for 5 minutes. Cool and sprinkle with almonds.

Rhubarb Marmalade

6 JARS

6 cups rhubarb, cut into ½-inch pieces
1 orange, very thinly sliced
6 cups sugar
2 tablespoons minced ginger root

Remove seeds from orange. Place rhubarb and orange in large saucepan and pour in sugar. Add ginger. Let stand 24 hours. Bring to a boil, then reduce heat and cook until thick and syrupy, about 40 minutes. It may take longer, but be careful it doesn't burn. Stir frequently. When mixture sheets from spoon, remove from heat and pour into sterilized jelly glasses. Seal, following the Instructions for Preserving on page 185.

Rhubarb and Strawberry Sherbet

1 QUART

2 cups rhubarb, finely chopped
2 cups fresh strawberries, chopped
1 cup sugar
½ cup honey
½ cup orange juice
2 tablespoons lemon juice
Grated rind of 1 lemon
2 egg whites
Pinch of salt
2 tablespoons sugar

Place fruit in saucepan and cook over medium heat for about 5 minutes, until juice runs. Stir in sugar, honey, juices and rind. Let cool. Pour into flat pan and put into freezer until mushy, about 2 hours. Spoon into bowl and whip until light. Beat egg whites with salt and 2 tablespoons sugar until stiff. Fold into rhubarb mixture. Return to freezer and stir up twice more at 2-hour intervals. Serve with crisp sugar cookies.

CHAPTER 7

_{::}

GRAPES

"Graft the tender shoot;
Thy children's children shall enjoy the fruit."
—Virgil

Perhaps nowhere in the orchard is that thought more truly proven than with the grapevine. These plants can live and go on bearing for as long as a hundred years, providing fruit for five generations until they are themselves an integral part of the history of a family. Indeed, we find the grape depicted in words, paintings and sculpture down through the ages, and it always seems to symbolize the good life—a tapestry of vineyards across a sun-warmed hillside; cascading bunches of ripe grapes to enjoy with cheeses, crusty breads and clear wines; the cool shade of an arbor on a hot summer's day; wine festivals with the colorful celebration of the harvest; all the stories of the Bible and mythology and twice-told tales that celebrate the grape and its rewards.

The one cultivar, or variety, most commonly grown in over two-thirds of the country (it responds to cooler weather as opposed to hot and arid weather) is the *Vitis labrusca*. This is the slipskin, or Concord type. The European *Vitis vinfera* is grown in California and Arizona and *Vitis rotundifolia* is the southern muscadine. You will have to decide whether you prefer to eat or drink your grapes because the table and the wine varieties are not interchangeable in their uses.

We have not attempted to grow wine grapes, preferring to leave that science to the experts; and after a trip through the Napa Valley I am convinced that we were right. Wine making is an exacting and definitive art and it is the wise man who knows in which direction his talents lie. The suburban wine-maker with a book in one hand and a beaker in the other is having fun, but must we drink it? We grow our grapes for their beauty, their flavor, their fragrance and the totally decorative effect of an arbor that provides a pleasing entrance to a small guest cottage on the hillside. We also grow them for jam, jelly, pies, tarts, salads, grape juice and a garnish for everything from soup to nuts. As if this isn't enough, we can brine the young leaves for Greek Dolmas or use them to line baskets and trays for al fresco dining.

A grapevine is a natural heritage to pass down to our children's children as it was passed down to us from our colonial ancestors. Long-lived and fruitful, it provides a bountiful blessing for the dedicated gardener.

SOIL

Grapes adapt to almost any kind of soil as long as the drainage is good; an average, not too rich, soil is best.

PLANTING AND BUILDING AN ARBOR

Decide what purposes your grapes are to achieve besides providing beautiful, edible fruits. They will have to be trained up onto some kind of support by the second year, such as an arbor, the side of the house or a fence. Do you want to define a property line, screen off an undesirable view, add privacy or mark an entrance to your garden or orchard? They must have full sun, so if your growing season is short it might be wise to put them against a south wall where they will get reflected heat. Good drainage and a gentle slope are ideal and they will thrive on it.

Late fall or early spring should see you out there digging holes about a foot deep and large enough to let the roots rest easily. Six to eight feet between plants is about the right distance and rows should be 10 feet apart. Add compost, bone meal or manure to the hole, mixing it well in with the soil. Set the plants in at the same depth as they were in the nursery and follow the usual procedure for tamping down and firming the soil. Cut the canes back to all but 2 buds, which brings us right into the pruning schedule.

By the time their second year has come around, you will have to build some kind of arbor. If you are not handy in the carpentry line, you can grow your grapevines simply on wires strung between posts, but grapes do lend themselves so definitely to an arbor setting that it is worthwhile to build one.

When we decided to build a grape arbor, a landscape architect gave us some helpful advice. She told us to drive around and look at different arbors for design and detail and then copy the one we especially liked for our own home. We did this and it was interesting to see how many different kinds of arbors there were and the various spots on which they were located. (We saw things in our own neighborhood that we'd never noticed before.) We finally narrowed the field down to the one we wanted and, as we were standing in the road sketching it, the owner came out, a bit curious as to exactly what we were doing. When we explained, he invited us to come in and inspect the arbor more closely, told us in detail just how it had been built and even recommended certain varieties of grapes. I was also given the recipe for his wife's grape juice which couldn't be easier and is as pure and fragrant as the grapes themselves.

If possible, place your arbor so that the prevailing winds run through it rather than against it.

This is the type of arbor we put up, allowing for the fact that we live on a windy hilltop and it had to be sturdy enough to resist the sudden gusts, occasionally up to 50 miles an hour. Use cedar or redwood posts—4 x 4 uprights, 8 feet high. Creosote (a process of rot prevention) the bottom 3 feet to prevent rot. Dig holes 2½ feet deep and sink 8 posts 6 to 8 feet deep—that is, 4 posts on each side. Onto the posts tack wooden slats running the length of the arbor. Tie the grapes to these slats. Plant the grapes halfway between the posts.

We happen to have a stone walk beneath the arbor. As nothing will grow there except weeds, you might cover the area with gravel or pine needles or make a brick path down the center and fill in the sides with pachysandra or any shade-growing ground cover. Spring bulbs add a cheery note blooming through the greenery.

MULCHING

Grapes prefer a well-mulched, weed-free area, but this is the rule rather than the exception for all of your food plants and bushes.

FERTILIZING

Grapes like potash, so if you've been making good use of your fireplace, you'll have lots of grapefeed on hand. You can also use manure or a commercial fertilizer. Feed in the spring and fall, spreading the fertilizer in a circular band 12 to 18 inches from the base of the plants.

PRUNING

Pruning is necessary for fuller grape production and with grapes it must be done ruthlessly. Do your pruning in late winter, which my professional gardening friend Sal Gilbertie says does *not* mean early spring.

- At planting time for the first year: prune canes back to 2 buds.

- The second year bind the stalk to the trellis with string or soft cloth. Prune off all growth except one cane and leave 4 to 5 buds on it.
- The third year leave 2 fruiting canes with 6 to 8 buds on them.
- The fourth year leave 2 longer fruiting canes with 10 to 12 buds on them.
- The fifth year leave 3 longer fruiting canes with 10 to 12 buds on them. From then on prune as for the fifth year, leaving 1 to 3 spurs for each fruiting cane.

A spur is a cane trimmed back to 2 buds. A bud is that part of the node which produces the fruiting shoot and the canes that grow from a spur will bear fruit the following year. Which canes do you leave? Choose those that have grown the previous year. As a rule of thumb, leave 4 canes per vine.

INSECTS AND DISEASES

Most home grape growers will agree that they are not troubled by too many problems of this nature. However, the birds can cause you a lot of frustration and do quite a bit of damage to your crop. There is one way around this menace—bagging the bunches.

Interestingly enough, grapes don't need direct sunlight to develop color in the berries. This is governed by the amount of sugars produced by the leaves and transferred to the fruits. Therefore, the leaves need the sunlight, and it is possible to reduce bird problems by bagging the fruit clusters. When the fruits are about half grown, tie brown paper bags over them securely to the canes. This will deflect both birds and harsh weather and give you generally better fruit quality at the same time.

Another interesting point about birds and grapes, and I do not know the answer to it, is that birds like the purples, blues and reds better than the white grapes. You take it from there.

177

A worry in the Northeast is the Japanese beetle, which comes and goes in cycles. For this you can simply catch the beetles in jars, put out bug traps or buy milky spore disease, which is advertised in organic and gardening magazines.

Black rot and mildews can be bothersome and they are especially virulent during a wet summer. These can be controlled by sprays or a prayer for dry weather.

There is a pest called the grape berry moth that is a small greenish larva that feeds in the berries. Usually this does not occur in large enough numbers to cause any real damage. Leaf hoppers, grape flea beetles and aphids are also part of the picture, but again, not prevalent enough to discourage you from planting grapes.

HARVESTING

Grapes must ripen on the vine and the best test for ripeness—in addition to color—is taste.

VARIETIES

EARLY SEASON

Buffalo: A heavy and regular bearer of sweet blue grapes. It's good for jams and jellies.

Fredonai: A blue-black grape with full clusters and a rich flavor.

Ontario: An early white grape that requires no spraying.

Van Buren: Good for its short growing season. It features large purple clusters that ripen in early September; of the Concord type.

MID-SEASON

Brighton: A sweet, highly flavored red grape; it is self-sterile.

Delaware: A good grape to pollinate with Brighton. It is a high quality red grape with good flavor.

Concord: This is probably the best-known grape. It is large, juicy and sweet and excellent for jelly, juice, and eating fresh.

Niagara: The most widely planted white grape; it is very productive. It features a beautiful amber-green-white color with a tangy Muscat flavor.

MUSCADINE FOR THE SOUTH

Higgins: An enormous white grape. It is best for wines and juices; matures in mid-season.

Hunt: An all-purpose, excellent-quality black grape, which ripens evenly and early. Good for pies, jellies, jams.

Scuppernong: The best-known and oldest variety. It has bronze, medium-large berries and has a good quality and distinctive flavor.

RECIPES

Mosaic Tart

SWEET TART PASTRY

1/2 cup butter
1 cup flour
1/4 cup finely chopped walnuts
3 tablespoons confectioners' sugar

Preheat oven to 425°. Put butter, flour, walnuts and sugar in large bowl. Mix together with fingertips until dough is crumbly. Turn dough into an 8-inch tart or pie pan and with heel of hand push into place, making a shell that is fairly thick

179

on the sides. Put shell in freezer for 30 minutes. Bake shell for 15 to 20 minutes until golden. Cool.

FILLING

1 package (8 ounces) cream cheese, softened
3 tablespoons orange juice concentrate
1 to 1½ cups grapes in 3 different colors, seeded and halved

Beat cream cheese with orange juice concentrate until creamy. Spread this mixture over bottom of tart shell. Arrange grape halves in decorative design over cream cheese mixture.

GLAZE

¼ cup currant jelly (see page 165)
1 tablespoon kirsch

Heat currant jelly with kirsch. When liquid, brush over grapes and cream cheese. Refrigerate until ready to serve.

Harvest Dressing

WILL STUFF A 12-POUND BIRD

4 cups cornbread crumbs
3 bananas, mashed
1 cup grapes, halved and seeded
2 apples, peeled and diced
2 oranges, peeled and sectioned
1 cup chopped walnuts
½ cup melted butter or margarine
½ cup chicken bouillon

Put crumbs in large bowl and gently mix in fruits and nuts. Pack mixture loosely into goose or turkey, moistening at intervals with butter and broth.

An Autumn Salad

6 SERVINGS

> 2 tablespoons unflavored gelatin
> ¼ cup cold water
> 1 cup cider
> ½ cup sugar
> 1½ cups ginger ale
> Juice of 1 lemon
> Pinch of salt
> 1 cup grapes, seeded and halved
> ½ cup grapefruit sections
> ½ cup orange sections
> Watercress to garnish

Soak gelatin in cold water. Heat cider to boiling and add sugar. Stir until sugar dissolves. Remove from heat and stir in dissolved gelatin. Add ginger ale, lemon juice and a pinch of salt. Chill mixture about 1 hour until syrupy, about the consistency of egg white. Combine with fruits and turn into a 5- to 6-cup ring mold. Chill for several hours or overnight. Unmold and surround with watercress. Serve with a mayonnaise–sour cream dressing thinned with fruit juice.

Mrs. Belden's Easy Grape Juice

1 QUART

> 1 cup grapes
> ½ cup sugar
> About 1 quart water, boiling

Into a sterilized quart jar (see page 185), put the grapes and sugar. Fill jar to the top with boiling water. Screw cap on jar and let stand in a cool place for a month or more. Turn the jar occasionally. Pour off juice, refrigerate it, and use it promptly.

Constance Spry Chicken Salad

6 SERVINGS

1 chicken (4 pounds), cooked and cooled
3 to 4 eggs, hard-cooked
2 celery hearts, cut into thin strips
1 green pepper, seeded and cut into thin strips
1 medium bunch large grapes, peeled and seeded (about
    ½ pound grapes)
Vinaigrette dressing flavored with mustard
Freshly ground black pepper to taste
½ cup blanched almonds, slivered
2 oranges, peeled and sectioned

Take meat from bones of chicken and cut into thin strips. Separate yolks and whites of eggs. Chop whites and sieve yolks. Into large bowl, put chicken, egg whites, celery, pepper and grapes. Toss all together in vinaigrette dressing. Arrange in center of serving dish and cover with sieved yolks. Grind fresh black pepper over all. Cover with slivered almonds. Arrange orange slices around the dish.

Chicken Livers and Grapes

4 SERVINGS

1 pound chicken livers
Flour to dust
4 tablespoons butter
2 tablespoons chopped shallots
Salt to taste
Freshly ground pepper to taste
½ teaspoon ground ginger
¼ cup chicken bouillon
¼ cup Marsala wine (dry)
1½ cups seedless grapes
½ cup sour cream

Dust chicken livers lightly with flour. Heat butter in large skillet. Add shallots and livers and sauté about 7 minutes or until brown on all sides. Add salt, pepper, ginger, bouillon, wine and half of grapes. Cover and cook for 5 to 7 minutes until livers are barely pink. Remove livers and grapes with slotted spoon to serving dish. Turn heat to high and reduce liquid in pan until slightly thickened. Stir in sour cream; pour sauce over livers. Garnish with remaining grapes and serve at once.

Concord Grape Pie

1 large bunch Concord grapes (2 pounds)
¾ cup sugar
1½ tablespoons flour
1 tablespoon butter
Pastry for two 8-inch piecrusts

Preheat oven to 450°. Slip skins off grapes. Put pulp in saucepan and skins in bowl. Cover saucepan and cook pulp until seeds separate from pulp, about 10 minutes. Place colander over bowl containing skins and pour in pulp from saucepan. Press pulp through colander into bowl, leaving seeds in colander. Mix skins and pulp with sugar and flour. Pour into pastrylined pie pan and dot with butter. Cover with top pastry crust. Bake for 10 minutes, then lower heat to 350° and bake 10 minutes longer.

Grape Jam

6 JARS (8 OUNCES EACH)

6 cups Concord grapes, stemmed
6 cups sugar

Put grapes and sugar into large kettle. Bring to a boil. Boil, stirring frequently, for 20 to 30 minutes until mixture thickens. Put through medium blade of food mill to remove seeds and skins. Pour into sterilized jars and seal, following the Instructions for Preserving on page 185.

Marjorie Mills' Muscatel Jelly

6 SERVINGS

1½ envelopes unflavored gelatin
½ cup cold water
1 cup boiling water
¼ teaspoon salt
1 cup sugar
1½ cups Muscatel wine
Juice of 1 large lemon
1 cup white seedless grapes
1 to 1½ cups sliced peaches (1 or 2 peaches)

Soften gelatin in cold water. Dissolve in boiling water. Add salt and sugar and stir until dissolved. Add wine and lemon juice. Blend well. Chill about 1 hour until partially congealed. Arrange grapes and peaches in a 5- to 6-cup mold and pour gelatin mixture over them. Chill several hours until firm. Serve as a salad with yogurt dressing or as a dessert with cream.

INSTRUCTIONS FOR PRESERVING

Once you have prepared jellies, jams and fruits to be preserved, it is important to put them in their containers and seal them properly. If you use a commercially made canning jar, be sure to follow the manufacturer's instructions for its use. In any case, your containers must be sterilized, and you must pack them properly.

To sterilize your containers, fill them $3/4$ full of water, place them in a shallow pan of water, and simmer them for 15 to 20 minutes. If you put the lids lightly on the containers, they will be sterilized at the same time. Keep the containers hot until you are ready to use them.

After you pour your preserves into their containers (which should be hot and dry), make sure that you wipe their rims and outsides to remove any splashes or spills. You must also remove all air bubbles from containers of fruit; you can use a thin spatula to pop the bubbles.

If the recipe calls for sealing, you must leave $1/4''$ between the preserve and the top of the jar. Sealing is done with paraffin that is melted over low heat or hot water. Pour a very thin layer of paraffin on top of the still-warm preserve and let it harden. Pour a second layer of paraffin (about $3/16''$ thick), tilting the container so the paraffin covers the entire surface. When the second layer is hard, put the lid on the container.

Store your jellies, jams and fruits in a cool, dry and dark place.

INDEXES

::
::

There is an index for each of the two subjects in this book—gardening and cooking. The gardening index, below, contains all entries relating to growing and caring for the orchard. The recipe index starts on page 188.

GARDENING

RECIPES